Ess
Alga
Southern Portugal

by
GERRY CRAWSHAW

Gerry Crawshaw is a highly experienced
travel writer. He writes for numerous
magazines and journals, and has also written
guides to a variety of countries.

C000319213

AA

Produced by AA Publishing

**Written by Gerry Crawshaw
Peace and Quiet section
by Paul Sterry**

Edited, designed and produced by AA Publishing. Maps © The Automobile Association 1994

Distributed in the United Kingdom by AA Publishing, Fanum House, Basingstoke, Hampshire, RG21 2EA.

The contents of this publication are believed correct at the time of printing. Nevertheless, the publishers cannot be held responsible for any errors or omissions, or for changes in details given in this guide or for the consequences of any reliance on the information provided by the same. Assessments of attractions, hotels, restaurants and so forth are based upon the author's own experience and, therefore, descriptions given in this guide necessarily contain an element of subjective opinion which may not reflect the publisher's opinion or dictate a reader's own experience on another occasion.
We have tried to ensure accuracy in this guide, but things do change and we would be grateful if readers would advise us of any inaccuracies they may encounter.

First published 1991
Revised Second edition 1993
Revised Third edition © The Automobile Association 1994

A CIP catalogue record for this book is available from the British Library.

ISBN 0 7495 0831 0

Published by AA Publishing, which is a trading name of Automobile Association Developments Limited, whose registered office is Fanum House, Basingstoke, Hampshire, RG21 2EA.
Registered number 1878835.

Colour separation: L. C. Repro, Aldermaston

Printed by: Printers Trento, S.R.L., Italy

Front cover picture: *Albufeira*

Country Distinguishing Signs

On several maps, international distinguishing signs indicate the location of countries that surround Portugal.
ⓔ = Spain

This book employs a simple rating system to help choose which places to visit:

✓	'top ten'

♦♦♦ do not miss
♦♦ see if you can
♦ worth seeing if you have time

The bay at Praia do Camilo, in Lagos: stunning scenery and blue skies

INTRODUCTION

Southern Portugal's premier tourist region is the Algarve, the country's southernmost province and one which was dominated for 500 years by the Moors, who came from North Africa in search of fertile land. They found an area warmed by the Gulf Stream, with 3,000 hours of sunshine a year – more than the Spanish Costa Brava, Majorca or the French Riviera – ideal for their orange groves, vineyards, almond and olive orchards. They named the land 'Al Gharb', and their influence can still be seen today, in the architecture, music and placenames of the area.

As well as Algarvian culture, there is more than 100 miles (160km) of rugged coastline with magnificent tide-washed golden sand beaches or tiny hidden coves for the sun worshipper. For the more energetic, the sporting facilities are excellent, in particular golf and tennis. Indeed, whichever resort you choose you are never far from a course or court, while the turquoise waters of the Atlantic are excellent for windsurfing and waterskiing,

First-time visitors to the Algarve are often surprised by its greenness and the profusion of wild flowers, especially in spring when the landscape is covered in delicate white almond blossom.

Traces of 500 years of Moorish occupation are to be found in the squat, whitewashed houses, intricately decorated chimney pots, brightly coloured fishing boats, and the *azulejos* – the ceramic coloured tiles which cover the walls of churches.

Algarve markets, too, are a revelation: colourful and noisy, they sell just about everything

imaginable, and no visit is complete without bargaining with the locals. Handicrafts widely available include attractive and good value ceramics, tiles, leather goods, copperware, cork, straw and cane products.

The larger resorts are well equipped for the visitor, with a wide range of accommodation to suit most tastes and pockets, discothèques and nightclubs, and good restaurants. Indeed, the choice of eating places is amazing.

Algarvian cuisine is simple yet delightful, with good supplies of fresh meat, fish and seafood, superb fruit and vegetables available all year, and all can be washed down with perfectly acceptable local wine.

Even though the Algarve remains the most popular holiday region within the country, with the widest range of hotels, attractive villas and apartments, and good tourist facilities, there is much more to southern Portugal.

To the northwest, for instance, lies the old province of Alentejo – 'beyond the Tagus' – which occupies a third of the total land area of Portugal, and which contains many fascinating cities, towns and villages popular as holiday destinations in their own right as well as being favourite excursion points for holiday-makers staying in the Algarve. These include Beja, capital of the Lower Alentejo, and Portalegre, capital of the Upper Alentejo.

Of particular interest to the visitor is the district of Estremadura, comprising the square-ended peninsula west of the Tagus estuary, with Portugal's capital, Lisbon, on its southern side. Good roads linking Lisbon with the extreme south mean that the capital is included in the excursion itineraries of many staying in the resorts bordering the Algarve's lovely beaches – and vice versa.

But those wishing to combine the shopping, sightseeing and nightlife attractions of cosmopolitan Lisbon with the relaxation of golden sands are by no means confined to Lisbon/Algarve combinations. Lisbon is unusual for a major European capital in that it offers two delightful coastal resorts practically on its doorstep: Estoril and neighbouring Cascais, both well equipped with excellent hotels, restaurants and other tourist amenities.

BACKGROUND

History

Like the rest of the southern
Iberian peninsula the Algarve
bears the unmistakable marks
left by 500 years of Moorish
domination, not only in Arabic
placenames such as Albufeira,
Faro or Benasfrim, but in its
architecture and in the
characteristics of its people.
It was in AD711 that the Moorish
invaders swept into the Algarve,
but they were by no means the
first to colonise the region. The
Cyretes first inhabited the
southern strip of coast, having
come to it from Andalucia; the
Phoenicians and Carthaginians
established fishing colonies; and
the ancient Greeks, in their turn,
visited the coast. It was,
however, the Romans who
organised the region,
establishing a proper irrigation
system, putting agriculture on a
properly planned basis, and

*A legacy of Roman occupation: the
Roman temple at Évora*

establishing minor cities in their
distinctive style. But once the
initial challenge had passed they
departed and left the region to
the Visigoths who occupied it
early in the 5th century. It was
the Visigoths' occupation that
was later interrupted by the
Moors.
The capital city of this Moorish
empire was Chelb, known today
as Silves. At the height of its
power it was a river port with
direct access to the sea, larger
and vastly more important than
Portugal's present capital city,
Lisbon. Its public buildings were
elegantly styled and in its garden
setting artists, writers and
philosophers flourished. In that
distant heyday, the city's
population topped 30,000, but its
value as a port diminished with
the silting up of the River Arade.
When Silves fell, so fell the

BACKGROUND

The castle at Silves, Moorish capital city

empire of the Moors. That turning point in history came in 1189 when Dom Sancho I, King of Portugal, persuaded German and English Crusaders to join him in an attack on the Moors, and the combined army laid siege to Silves. It lasted from mid-July until the beginning of September in that year and resulted in the conquest and pillaging of the city.

Though Faro and part of the coastline remained under Moorish domination for another 60 years, the fall of Silves marked the end of an era. From that time the rulers of Portugal called themselves 'Kings of Portugal and the Algarve', unconsciously emphasizing the region's separate identity.

The Algarve came to prominence in the 15th century when Prince Henry the Navigator established his 'think-tank' at Sagres. It was he who despatched his captains on their monumental voyages of discovery, and in the course of a single century Portugal discovered and explored nearly two-thirds of the inhabited globe. The country's contribution to man's knowledge of his planet stands unequalled and it is one of the sad ironies of history that Henry himself died before the greatest of these discoveries. He certainly laid the foundations of Portuguese seamanship and navigation which led to the discovery of Brazil and the Azores and eventually to Vasco da Gama's voyage round Africa to India.

Around this time developed the highly decorative late Gothic style of architecture known as Manueline, after King Manuel I (1495–1521). It derives its inspiration from the Discoveries and its chief characteristics are coral, seaweed, ropes and anchors carved in stone.

Until the 15th century the Algarve was almost totally isolated from the rest of Europe, and, in fact, from the rest of Portugal. The activities of Prince Henry helped in some measure to break this isolation, but cut off from the north by the Caldeirão and Monchique mountains and separated from Spain by the Guadiana river, it developed in its own way and at its own pace. But not even the Algarve, 150 miles (240km) from Lisbon, could escape the devastating earthquake which wiped out much of the capital in 1755. Whole Algarvian communities were killed and many churches and houses were destroyed; the region's own capital, Faro, was ruined for a second time in a generation, having barely recovered from an earlier earthquake which had struck in 1722. Slowly, however, the Algarve recovered, although until the end of World War II it remained virtually unknown outside Portugal. Since then, the Algarve's holiday attributes – a delightful climate coupled with incomparable beaches – have become appreciated far and wide, making the region one of the most popular holiday destinations in Europe for the past 20 or so years.

Inevitably, this popularity has led to problems. Keen to cash in on the tourist boom, developers were once given a virtually free hand to build where and how they liked. The result was that what were once small, picturesque fishing ports fringing lovely stretches of golden sand were totally transformed, with scant regard for the environment, into sprawling holiday resorts.

The Portuguese government is well aware of the damage that has been caused and, at last, has introduced stricter laws governing further tourist development. Some argue that the damage has already been done, but while it cannot be denied that several resorts have

The Great Discoveries are celebrated in style, in Lisbon's elegant monument

been allowed to develop more than is good for them, the region as a whole continues to offer many delightful and relatively unspoiled resorts equipped with excellent hotels and restaurants and ample tourist facilities.

Prince Henry the Navigator (1394–1460)

The fourth son of King John I of Portugal and Philippa, daughter

BACKGROUND

of John of Gaunt, Henry was born at Oporto and rose to prominence in the North African expedition which culminated in the fall of Ceuta in 1415. During this campaign his attention was almost certainly drawn for the first time to the possibilities for expansion and commerce afforded by the African continent. He would have had opportunities for gathering information on the lucrative traffic in gold, slaves and other commodities, which for centuries had been maintained by caravans operating between the Niger region and the ports of North Africa. His early motives, however, were more probably to cripple Moorish power, to extend the boundaries of the known world and to convert the heathen to Christianity. The economic motive became more powerful later, when the sea-route to west Africa outflanked the land-routes under Moorish control.

The early 15th century was a significant time in Portugal's efforts at expansion overseas, and Henry's residence at Sagres soon became a centre for Portuguese maritime enterprise: there he consulted with navigators and cartographers and assembled the best available charts and aids to navigation (see page 47–48). The first stage was the rediscovery of Madeira and Porto Santo by Gonçalves Zarco in 1419–20, followed by that of the Azores. A series of fruitless attempts to round Cape Bojador followed until, in 1434, Gil Eanes succeeded. Two years later,

the Rio do Oro was reached and gold and slaves obtained for the first time.

The advance then became rapid; in 1443 Nuno Tristão reached the bay of Arguin, where a trading fort was established; in 1445 Zarco rounded Cape Verde; and during the next decade Portuguese seamen and traders were frequenting the mouths of the Gambia and the Rio Grande, and the Cap Verde Islands were discovered.

Because of troubles at home, the pace of discovery then slackened but by the time of Henry's death in 1460 the Portuguese were approaching Sierra Leone. After his death the direction was assumed by the crown of Portugal and carried to ultimate success by the establishment of a sea route to the Indies and Portugal's first steps on the road to wealth and empire.

THE ALGARVE

ALBUFEIRA ✓

The Romans were in Albufeira: they called it Baltum and built a fort there. Later the Visigoths came and went and then, in the 8th century, the Moors, who changed its name to Al-Buhera (Castle-on-the-Sea). It was then a prosperous town, mainly because of a flourishing trade with North Africa.
Occupied by the Christians in 1189 and lost two years afterwards, it was the Knights of St James who reconquered it in the middle of the 13th century, during the reign of King Afonso III, although the loss of trade with Morocco almost ruined it. Then a fishing village for centuries, it was raised to the status of town in 1504, and was visited by King

Albufeira's fishing boats show the other side of life in this busy resort

Sebastião in 1573, when it already had an important castle equipped with artillery to defend it against the Moorish, French and English corsairs who at that time used to harass the coast of the Algarve. The 1755 earthquake practically destroyed the town and, in 1833, it was set on fire by guerrillas, after a siege and a battle.
Today, Albufeira – about 24 miles (38.6km) west of Faro – is the premier resort of the region, sometimes flatteringly referred to as 'the St Tropez of the Algarve'. Built on a hill with narrow streets and a cliff-top walk, it is an interesting resort, retaining at least some of the charm of a picturesque fishing village in spite of recent hotel, villa and apartment development.

THE ALGARVE

Beaches

Below the town, reached either by steps or by a tunnel that penetrates the cliff face, is the chief reason for the resort's popularity – its excellent sandy beach. Backed by the familiar red cliffs upon which the town has been built, it is clean and safe, and suitable for family bathing.

The east end of the beach also serves as a harbour for numerous brightly painted fishing boats, and a free tourist attraction is provided each evening here by the fishermen who manhandle their boats down the beach and launch them into the surf.

Flanking the town are other beaches, all have safe paths leading down from the road. São Rafael is recommended; the first good beach going west, it has impressive rock formations. Going east is Olhos d'Água (see page 40–41), and the nearest, Baleeira, is attractive and popular with the locals. There are other small beaches at Castelo and Galé. Albufeira is well positioned for visits to all the resorts along the coast, either by car or local bus.

Many hotels advertised by tour operators as being in Albufeira are, in fact, in the Praia da Oura

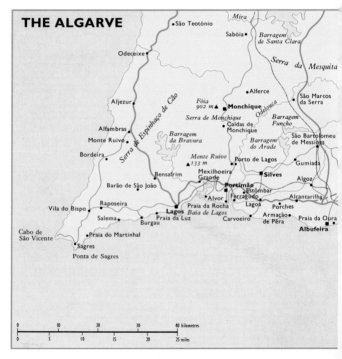

(see page 44–45) and São João districts, about 2 miles (3km) from Albufeira.

The main beach at Albufeira is safe and sandy, and marvellous for family holidays

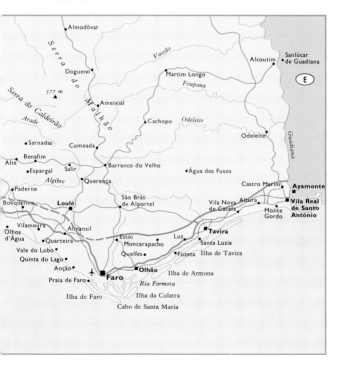

One of Albufeira's four churches

Old Town

Balconied houses with caged canaries in windows and doorways, and narrow whitewashed lanes and arches give a Moorish feel to the old town. From the square called Praça dos Barcos there are lovely views of Albufeira and of the beach.

Sightseeing

Churches

Of particular interest to the visitor are four churches: Santana, whose minaret-decorated dome gives it a Byzantine feel; the Chapel of the Misericórdia, originally built in the 16th century and subsequently reconstructed; Matriz, the parish church, reconstructed after the 1755 earthquake; and the church of São Sebastião.

Statue of Vicente de Carvalho

Located in the centre of town, in Largo Jacinto d'Ayet, this honours Albufeira's most famous son. A one-time Augustinian friar, he was arrested in Japan during a period of brutal Christian repression in the 1630s. He was subsequently burned at the stake in Nagasaki but later beatified in his native Portugal in the 19th century.

Town Hall

The town hall is one of the resort's most striking buildings, resembling a church with its fine, open ironwork belfry.

Xorino Grotto

A curious rock formation, this is especially interesting if approached by boat.

Paderne

Paderne, which is approximately 8 miles (13km) from Albufeira, is a picturesque old village with a parish church containing valuable images and altar-pieces in carved wood. There is also a ruined castle and the ruins of a Gothic church.

Porches

At Porches, the Olaria Pequena ('little earthenware') pottery produces beautiful individual pieces. On the other side of the road a little further towards Lagoa, the main Olaria shop is also recommended.

Tourist Information: Rua 5 de Outubro (tel: (089) 512144).

Accommodation

Hotel da Aldeia (tel: (089) 588861). A medium-sized, modern hotel forming part of a large villa/apartment complex within five minutes of the beach and about a mile (2km) from Albufeira. Its swimming pool, set in a busy sun terrace, is also used by villa and apartment guests. There are pleasant gardens and a poolside bar, children's pool and playground, restaurant with à la carte menus available, discothèque and live music most nights, a card room, satellite television, video, table tennis, mini golf and tennis.

Hotel Alfa Mar (tel: (089) 501224). A large, modern hotel opposite the beach in Praia da Falésia, about six miles (9.5km) from Albufeira, the Alfa Mar is set in extensive grounds leading down to the beach.

Hotel Apartamento Auramar Areias de São João (tel: (089) 587607). Located at Praia da Oura, nearly three miles (4.5km) from Albufeira, the Auramar is within five minutes' walk from the beach, reached by steep steps. It is split into four blocks, with excellent sea views from its headland position. Closed November to March.

Hotel Boa Vista (tel: (089) 589175). This small, modern hotel is situated 15 minutes from the beach and slightly less from the centre of Albufeira in a quiet residential area.

Hotel Califórnia Rua Cândido dos Reis (tel: (089) 586833): a well run hotel in the centre of Albufeira.

Clube Mediterranée (tel: (089) 512681). Above the beach at Praia de Balaia, 4 miles (6.5km) east of Albufeira, with access via steep steps, the hotel is set in beautiful grounds that offer excellent sports facilities. The swimming pool is set in a pleasant sun terrace/garden area, and there is also a children's pool and playground,

plus a poolside bar.

Hotel Montechoro (tel: (089) 589423). Situated at the top of the hill of Montechoro looking towards the sea, about 3 miles (5km) east of Albufeira. This hotel has 314 rooms and 48 suites all with private bath, balcony and air-conditioning.

Hotel Rocamar (tel: (089) 586990). A medium sized hotel situated right on the beach, with access to the beach down a long flight of steps.

Hotel Sol e Mar Rua José, Bernardino de Sousa (tel: (089) 586721). Above the beach, very close to the centre of Albufeira, this has a small swimming pool, discothèque with live music nightly and a gift shop.

Aparthotel Vila Magna Montechoro (tel: (089) 586611). An excellent modern apartment block in a large complex containing a variety of underground shops and cinema, the Vila Magna is located in the Montechoro district, about 3 miles (5km) from Albufeira, with an excellent beach about one and a half miles (2.5km) away at Praia da Oura.

Residência Villa Recife Rua Miguel Bombarda 6 (tel: (089) 586747). A delightful family-owned hotel converted from an old mansion on a main road within two minutes' downhill walk to the beach, and the same from the centre of Albufeira.

Restaurants

Albufeira offers numerous restaurants, many of them quite inexpensive, lining narrow streets, congregated around the square, or perched on the cliff-tops with fabulous views over the ocean. There are particularly good places just out of town at Olhos d'Agua, Olhos da Balaia and Castelo do Bispo.

A Ruína, next to the fish market, serves excellent seafood in a rustic setting, and the **Cabaz da Praia**, in Praça Miguel Bombarda, offers diners excellent French cuisine with a Portuguese accent, plus lovely sea views. **Sir Harry's Bar** is an English pub off the main square and is very popular and lively. There are almost as many bars as there are restaurants – disco bars, video bars and karaoke bars – and the occasional establishment where you can sit with a drink simply watching the sea and the stars.

Shopping

Albufeira is widely regarded as one of the best places for shopping in the Algarve, with an excellent selection of shops, market stalls and handicrafts. A large open-air market also runs throughout the summer months, starting near the main square and gradually winding down through countless narrow back streets. Saturday morning is traditionally the best time for the

Quality leather bags and purses are excellent value

market when the variety of goods on offer reaches its height. Quality local produce, including fruit, vegetables, cheeses and handicrafts are always on offer. Country fairs are held in the town on 4 February, 15 August and 29 November.

ALCOUTIM

Alcoutim, a river port on the banks of the Guadiana, is experiencing a new awakening thanks to its discovery by international tourists. Occupied by the Greeks, Phoenicians and Carthaginians, it was given the name of Alcoutinium by the Romans, while the Arabs came to dominate this important strategic position in the 8th century and were only expelled in 1240. Alcoutim is faced by Sanlúcar de Guadiana, its Spanish reflection across the water, and while Alcoutim, with its denticulated chimney-pots, is typically Algarve, Sanlúcar is no less typically Spanish, and the juxtaposition of two cultures separated by a fairly narrow stretch of water is curious. Both villages are dominated by ruined stone fortresses which have been glaring at one another for hundreds of years.

It was here, on boats anchored in the river, that King Fernando I of Portugal and King Henrique II of Castile signed the Peace of Alcoutim in 1371, thus ending the war between the two countries.

The town was associated with the Order of St James from the 14th century, but subsequently declined in importance and size.

Sightseeing

Worth seeing in Alcoutim are the parish church, with a Renaissance-style portal and columns with lovely capitals; the church of Nossa Senhora da Conceição, containing an interesting 18th-century altar-piece. Also, a ruined castle here provides excellent views of the town and the River Guadiana, with Spain on the opposite shore.

ALJEZUR

Originally settled by the Arabs in the 10th century, Aljezur was conquered in 1246 by the Master of the Order of St James, Dom Pedro Peres Correia, and was granted a town charter by Dom Dinis in 1280. But due to its situation in the mountainous interior of the Algarve, history has tended to pass it by. Today, it is appreciated by those visitors looking for relaxation and peace in tranquil surroundings with the sea in the background.

Sightseeing

Among the sites worth visiting are the parish church built in the 19th century and containing a remarkable statue of Our Lady of Dawn, and the castle, ruined by the 1755 earthquake, but nevertheless offering magnificent views over the surrounding countryside. Nearby is the picturesque village of Odeceixe, on the banks of a stream, and the quiet beaches of Samoqueira, Carriagen, Penedo and Vale Figueira.

Tourist Information: Largo do Mercado (tel: (082) 98229).

> **Algarve Chimneys**
> At Almansil, and indeed in most other towns in the Algarve, the chimneys are an attractive feature. All are individual, and the most ornate examples feature elaborate and fanciful perforated patterns – an unexpected and delightful aspect of the domestic architectural scene.

◆◆◆
ALMANSIL

The big attraction here is the nearby **Church of São Lourenço de Matos**, notable for its *azulejos* (tiles). The church is beautifully sited on a low hill, standing just above the main road. In the vestry, an ante-room to the chapel, are three 18th-century primitive oil paintings of contemporary miracles attributed to St Lawrence, the patron saint of the church. One is of a child falling unharmed from the window of a house in Faro. In the chapel itself the walls, from floor to ceiling, are faced with blue tiles depicting scenes from the life of St Lawrence, and the ceiling too is covered with blue *azulejos.*

Other points of interest include a gold baroque altar, and an impressive crucifixion group on the south wall. Adjoining the church is a Cultural Centre containing a stylish art gallery. Almansil is also the site of one of the Algarve's three water pleasure parks. At Wet 'n Wild you can spend the whole day on great water-slides, surf-pools, rapids and several other water-based amusements.

Restaurants
Delicious French and Swiss cuisine can be enjoyed at the **Casa da Torre Ermitage**, where booking is usually essential (tel: (089) 394329). **Pituxa**, on the old road to Vale de Lobo (400 yards, 450m) before the T-junction, is an excellent restaurant.

◆
ALTURA

Altura can hardly be described as a resort, but does have a beautiful, long and unspoilt beach, making it a good choice for an away-from-it-all beach holiday with few distractions. There is little of interest in the village itself, and scant shopping or nightlife, but Monte Gordo is only three miles (4.8km) away and can be reached by local bus, as can Faro, which lies 31 miles (50km) to the west.

Accommodation
Eurotel Altura (tel: (081) 956450): good facilities for children are among the features of this 3-star hotel, which has a sizeable play area, cots and high chairs, early meal arrangements if required, and a baby-sitting service. The hotel has a large swimming pool, and is situated by the beach between Monte Gordo and Tavira.

Restaurants
There are a few reasonably-priced local tavernas in the village, but those seeking really good, authentic Algarve fare should make a trip to **The Stable**, at Praia da Manta Rota, a fishing village a little further along the coast. Specialities here include Portuguese beef steak, Algarve cockles, lobster and crab.

◆◆
ALVOR

Alvor is a schizophrenic sort of place – a delightful unspoiled old village winds down cobbled streets to a characterful quay, while a short distance away, on its wide sandy beach, monolithic tower blocks scar the skyline with piecemeal developments straggling around them.

Alvor's recorded history dates from 1189 when the Crusaders, arriving by sea, killed several thousand occupying Moors in the cause of Christianity. It is believed, however, that the Carthaginian general Hannibal founded a settlement here. Dom João II (1481–95) made it a municipality and came here in 1495 on his way to take the waters at the inland spa of Caldas de Monchique.

Accommodation

Hotel Alvor-Praia (tel: (082) 458900). Its extensive facilities include a large swimming pool set in a garden and sun terrace area, tennis courts and sports equipment for hire, a poolside bar, spacious and attractive air-conditioned public areas, a large dining room, enjoying a good reputation and a grill room with regular dinner-dances.

Hotel Delfim (tel: (082) 458901). The hotel has 312 air-conditioned rooms, most with sea views, balcony and private bath. There is an extensive range of facilities including an attractive swimming pool area, restaurant and tennis courts, and a good activity and entertainment programme.

Hotel Dom João II (tel: (082) 459135). A large, modern hotel situated opposite the beach and

The luxurious Hotel Alvor-Praia caters for the visitor's every need, and has good views

forming the centrepiece of the Torralta holiday complex, the Dom João II has a medium-size swimming pool with a section for children, poolside bar, children's playground, and comfortable public areas.

Hotel do Golfe da Penina (tel: (082) 415415): this beautiful, 5-star hotel is located 4 miles (6.4km) from Praia de Alvor – to which a courtesy bus operates – and is about 2 miles (3km) from Alvor itself, in a secluded position within the famous Henry Cotton-designed golf course, making it an attractive proposition for golfers.

THE ALGARVE

Restaurants
The **Al-Vila**, at Sitio das Amoreiras, enjoys an excellent reputation, while **Barca de Alvor**, on the beach, is also popular, especially in the evenings.

◆◆
ARMAÇÃO DE PÊRA
About 27 miles (43.5km) west of Faro, Armação de Pêra has an excellent, large beach set against a dramatic backdrop of

The pleasant old parts of Armação de Pêra can still be found among the high-rise apartments and hotels

huge sandstone cliffs. Unfortunately it is suffering the same fate as many other once unspoilt villages in the Algarve, with cranes and bulldozers creating yet more holiday hotels, villas and apartments. There is, as yet, little in the way of shopping or nightlife in Armação de Pêra, but the busy resort of Albufeira is only five miles (8km)

away, and it is well placed for excursions by bus or car to the rest of the Algarve.

Sightseeing
Places of interest include a chapel dedicated to St Antony. Zoo Marine (performing dolphin and seals and parrot park) to the northeast, and the grottoes, caves and vaults at Furnas, reached by boat excursion, are also worth visiting.

Capela de Nossa Senhora da Rocha (Chapel of Our Lady of the Rocks)
Lying a short distance west of Armação de Pêra and set at the tip of a headland 100 feet (30m) above sea level, this chapel is reminiscent of those small Greek basilicas that guard the island harbours of the Aegean. Small, white and extremely simple, it has a curious shape, being hexagonal and crowned by a squat pyramid spire. Some Roman ruins are nearby. The chapel's tiny interior is dominated by painted wooden effigies of the Virgin and Child, and the walls are lined with wooden models of trawlers and fishing boats – sailors' thanksgiving offerings for vessels that have been saved at sea.

Tourist Information: Avenida Marginal (tel: (082) 312145).

Accommodation
Hotel Do Levante (tel: (082) 314900). This small, modern hotel, a 15-minute walk from Armação de Pêra, is above the superb beach; access by steps.
Hotel Do Garbe (tel: (082) 312187). A medium-size modern hotel opposite the beach.
Hotel Viking, Senhora da Rocha

Peaceful, whitewashed Burgau has an attractive setting

(tel: (082) 312336). A medium-size hotel above the beautiful twin beaches of Senhora da Rocha, 2.5 miles (4.5km) from Armaçáo de Pêra.

Restaurants
Good seafood can be enjoyed at the **Grelha**, at Rua do Alentejo 2, while **A Santola**, in Largo 25 de Abril, commands excellent views of the beach and can usually be relied upon for its simple cuisine.

◆◆
BURGAU
Burgau is an ancient fishing village, built on a hillside overlooking a horseshoe bay, and with a lovely beach of soft, golden sand.
Although relatively uncommercialised, the village has been steadily growing in popularity over the last few years and can now cater for most visitors' everyday needs, with several mini markets and tiny tourist shops. There is also an extremely varied scattering of restaurants, supplying anything from simple, inexpensive meals to excellent cuisine.
Just outside the village is Majek's Discothèque, the locals having thoughtfully placed it out of earshot of their homes. Here, also, is the British-run Burgau Sports Centre where sports enthusiasts are well catered for with tennis and squash courts, and on the beach there is windsurfing and waterskiing. There is also a local riding stable.
For those looking for something a little different, John Measures, an Englishman who has set up home in the Algarve, offers full day birdwatching trips to the

It can be very rough and extremely windy at the exposed promontory of Cape St Vincent

marshes and hills around the area, which hold a variety of wildfowl and waders (see also pages 85–91).

For gentler pursuits, half a mile (0.8km) outside the village lies the Burgau Arts Centre. Here, in a 200-year-old converted farmhouse, you can enjoy either photographic or art holidays, instructed by resident tutors.

Restaurant

Among the best restaurants in Burgau is **A Laranja**, which specialises in Portuguese and international dishes (tel: (082) 69234).

◆◆
CABO DE SÃO VICENTE (CAPE ST VINCENT)

Cape St Vincent was dubbed by ancient sailors 'O Fim do Mondo' (the End of the World) and it is easy to understand why. The ancient name for the Cape was Promontorium Sacrum (the Sacred Cape), from which Sagres, the peninsula to the east, derives its name. At Promontorium Sacrum the gods were supposed to rest at night after the labours of the day.

The Cape owes its present name to the legend that it was here that the corpse of St Vincent, an Italian martyr who died in 304, was washed ashore. His body was kept in the Church of the Ravens – so called because of the ravens that sheltered in its eaves – which stood on the site of the present chapel. The body of St Vincent was eventually taken to Lisbon and buried there in 1173; it is for this reason that ravens are emblazoned on the arms of the Portuguese capital. Another popular legend says that ravens accompanied the boat that took the body of St Vincent to Lisbon.

As Cape St Vincent commands the route from northern waters to the Mediterranean it is not surprising that many sea battles have been fought off it. In 1693 the French Admiral Tourville defeated a British fleet in these waters; Rodney beat the Spaniards here in 1780; while in 1797 it was the scene of a famous victory by Jarvis and Nelson when, with 15 ships, they routed a Spanish fleet of 27.

The light itself is said to be the most powerful in Europe, throwing a warning beam to approaching ships up to 60 miles (96.5km) out to sea.

◆◆◆
CARVOEIRO

The former fishing village of Carvoeiro lies about 37 miles (60km) from Faro Airport and 3 miles (5km) from Lagoa. It is wedged into a narrow valley with high red cliffs rising steeply and culminates in a tiny picturesque beach. In summer this is brim-full of sunbathers, marking their patches in between the fishing boats which still haul up on the beach here. There is nothing of historic interest in Carvoeiro, but the bright whitewashed houses and pretty café terraces lend an undeniable charm to this increasingly commercialised spot. To the east of here are more beautiful coves with some unspoiled beaches.

Just outside the resort, off Highway 125, is Slide and Splash, a popular aquapark.

Tourist Information: Largo da Praia (tel: (082) 357728).

Accommodation

Most of the accommodation is located at Praia do Carvoeiro comprising in the main, villa and apartment complexes, one of the best is the **Apartamento Solférias** (tel: (082) 357401), which is spacious and attractively laid out.

One of the main hotels in the town is the **Dom Sancho** in the main square (tel: (082) 357301), a fairly modest establishment with few frills.

Restaurants/Entertainment

Recommended restaurants include **Teodoro's,** on Rampa Nossa Senhora da Encarnaçao 9 (the street up from the beach to the chapel) (tel: (082) 357864), while east of Carvoeiro is **Restaurant Centianes**, at the lovely small cliff beach of Playa de Centianes, and with a view of the rock formations (tel: (082) 358724). For light meals and music in Carvoeiro try **Bar Whispers** on the main square.

THE ALGARVE

◆ CASTRO MARIM

Castro Marim is a small village near the River Guadiana and is dominated by fortresses standing on twin hills. Archaeological finds indicate that primitive man inhabited the height on which Castro Marim is situated, and which was probably an island in those times. The Phoenicians subsequently used it as a port and possibly founded the present settlement. A crossroads in Roman times, Castro Marim was an important centre during the Arab domination, while after the Christian reconquest it became part of the so-called Kingdom of the Algarve and received its municipal charter.

Sightseeing

Churches

The Church of Santo António contains an interesting altarpiece recalling the saint's miracles;

The old town of Castro Marim has fine examples of Algarvian architecture

the Church of São Sebastião contains a lovely 17th-century retable.

Fortresses

The principal fortress of Castro Marim belongs to the period of Afonso III, and was heavily restored in 1940 by the Portuguese government. Inside the impressive outer battlements there is another, smaller, castle – the *castelo velho*, which dates from about 1270. The great walls of the keep also enclose a ruined church, the remains of an 18th-century armoury, and an archaeological museum. The view from the battlements of the *castelo velho* is not to be missed. Across the river, on the Spanish side, a crumbling Moorish fort keeps watch from a hill in the distance. The fortress of São Sebastião lies on the other side of the village.

Marshland Reserve

Also of interest to bird-watchers is the Reserva Natural do Sapal de Castro Marim, taking in the marshy area surrounding the town which is rich in fauna and flora.

◆◆◆ FARO ✓

The busy commercial town, port and holiday resort of Faro lies at the northern end of a lagoon dotted with islands, about 186 miles (299km) from Lisbon and 32 miles (52km) from the frontier with Spain. It is the district capital of the Algarve and one of the region's most interesting and authentically Portuguese centres. Its international airport, lying 4 miles (7km) southwest, has made

it a focal point for the Algarve, but relatively few tourists explore the city's many attractions. The focal point of Faro is the Praça de Dom Francisco Gomes, named after an 18th-century bishop who was responsible for a considerable amount of building in Faro, including the beautiful Arco da Vila, an arched gateway crowned by a statue of Thomas Aquinas. One side of the square, which has a garden in the middle, is bounded by the docks, and ornamenting the square is an obelisk 49 feet (15m) high, commemorating the diplomat Ferreira de Almeida. From the Praça Francisco Gomes one enters the old town, hidden behind the remains of the Moorish wall, via the Arco da Vila. Through the gateway is the magnificent cathedral square

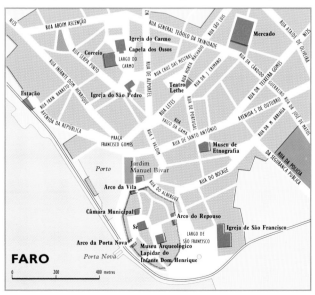

The lovely Arco da Vila, once the door to the old castle

flanked by the old episcopal palace. The convent here is now the Prince Henry Archaeological Museum.

Beach

Reached by the bridge or by ferry from the Porta Nova Quay, the Praia de Faro is the town's nearest beach. It is massive, and the islet helps form a sheltered, picture-postcard lagoon between it and the mainland. The far side is rather exposed and there are places where the water shelves steeply. Windsurfing and waterskiing are normally available here and there are all the usual deckchairs and sunloungers for hire, too. It is a popular spot which accordingly becomes very crowded during the summer season. On the Ilha da Barreta there is a lighthouse.

Sightseeing
Igreja do Carmo (Carmelite Church)

This interesting Baroque-style building stands in Largo do Carmo, near Faro's main post office. Its two large towers are visible from quite a distance, rising up over a wide façade and looking down upon the rest of the sprawling town. The giltwork is particularly impressive, as are the 18th-century wood carvings and an imposing statue of Our Lady of Mount Carmel by the 18th-century sculptor Machado de Castro.

From the Igreja do Carmo you can enter Faro's most intriguing place of interest, the **Capela dos Ossos** (Chapel of Bones), built in the last century. What gives it its macabre appeal is that it is lined with the skulls and bones of human skeletons. Apparently an over-enthusiastic 19th-century bishop used more than 1,200 skulls from monks buried in the old Carmo cemetery in the construction of the chapel, considering human skulls both cheaper and preferable as building materials than traditional bricks and stonework.
Open: Monday to Friday, 10.00–12.00hrs and 15.00–17.00hrs. Admission free.

Sé (Cathedral)

The cathedral is a curious, squat building with exposed bells. A huge mosque, built by the Moors a thousand years ago, originally stood on the site of the structure, which was started immediately after the invaders were forced out in the 13th century. Only the portico and tower remain of the original Gothic structure, the remainder being a mixture of baroque and Renaissance architectural designs heavily remodelled after the 1755 earthquake.

The interior is impressive, with a splendid barrel-roof and two fine chapels on each side of the high altar: the Chapel of the Holy Sacrament, a mass of carved figures, and the Chapel of the Relics, wonderful a blaze of rococo gold.

Also impressive are the 17th-century *azulejos* in the Chapel of Our Lady of the Rosary, in the southwest corner.

Open: Monday to Friday 10.00–12.00hrs. Admission free.

Igreja de São Francisco (Church of St Francis)

To the east of the cathedral rises the Arco do Repouso, one of the old town gates, which gives access to the spacious Largo de São Francisco. Here the 17th-century Church of St Francis contains large panels of tiles, glazed white and blue, recording the saint's life. The unique feature of this single-aisled church is the central octagon, rising to a dome at the entrance to the chancel. The walls are covered with exquisite baroque gold work, and there are altars at each corner with carved statues of saints.

Open: No official hours (check with the tourist office before visiting). Admission free.

Museu Arqueológico Lapidar do Infante Dom Henrique (Prince Henry Archaeological Museum)

Housed in the restored Convent of Nossa Senhora da Assunção,

The Chapel of Bones is a grisly place popular with visitors

this simple museum contains archaeological remains from the Roman and pre-Roman eras, religious paintings, a small section that is devoted to military memorabilia, and an enormous 19th-century bishop's chair. The most spectacular exhibit is a completely reconstructed Roman mosaic more than 30 feet (9m) long, which was unearthed from a nearby house during the construction of a sewer. The mosaic is in a room of its own and features a magnificent bearded sea god in its centre. Other rooms contain collections of pre-historic tools and weapons, mostly found locally, in addition to numerous statues discovered during excavations near the village of Estói, a little way inland.

Open: Monday to Friday,

09.30–12.30hrs and 14.00–17.30hrs. Admission charge.

Jesuit College

The former Jesuit College has been restored and contains a small, untouched 18th-century opera house, built by the Bivar family after the Jesuits had been suppressed in Portugal in the middle of the 18th century. (Not open.)

Old Town

The Old Town is the pleasantest part of Faro to wander in. Here are the mansions of the rich alongside the homes of the poor. Most of the shops and smart cafés and restaurants lie outside this area. In the eastern part of the town, on a hill commanding far-ranging views, stands the little church of Santo António do Alto (1754), with a museum devoted to St Antony. From the top of the hill there is an extensive panorama of the coastal lagoons.

Milreu

About 5 miles (8km) north of Faro, near the village of Estói, are the knee-high remains of a Roman villa, where excavations carried out from 1876 onwards brought to light baths with mosaic pavements, the apse of a 3rd-century church, mosaics, and shattered columns. Many of the remains are in the museum in Faro, and further excavations are being undertaken by a German team. (Closed Mondays; admission free).

Palace of Estói

Nearby is a charming late 18th-century country mansion , the Palace of Estói with formal gardens. Flights of steps with pools and statutory lead up to the terrace on which stands the elegant pink façade of the house. Only the gardens are open to the public, but a visit here is highly recommended.

Tourist Information: Rua da Misericórdia 8-12 (tel: (089) 803604).

Accommodation

Estalagem Ilhamar (tel: (089) 817542). This 4-star *estalagem* is in a good position on the island of Praia de Faro, which is linked to the mainland by a causeway. The beach – which shelves very quickly, making it not the best choice for those with small children – is just across the road, while at the rear of the hotel is the Rio Formosa, a calm inlet which is ideal for youngsters. The sheltered inlet provides good safe swimming while older children and adults can enjoy windsurfing on the island shore, which compensates for the lack of a swimming pool. The only disadvantage is that, since the airport is only 2 miles (3km) away, there can occasionally be aircraft noise.

Hotel Eva (tel: (089) 803354). A modern hotel in the centre of Faro, about 5 miles (8km) from the main beach area, with sea and harbour views from the front. Free bus service in summer to Faro Island beach.

Hotel Faro (tel: (089) 803276). Close to the centre of the town, overlooking the harbour, lagoon, islands and sea, it has 52 air-conditioned rooms.

The Largo da Sé (Cathedral Square) is a delightful space in the old town

Casa de Lumena (tel: (089) 801990). At Praça Alexandre Herculano 27; with only 12 rooms – all with bath – a delightful little hotel, formerly a ducal residence.

Monte do Casal (tel: (089) 91503). close to the village of Estói, north of Faro, this small 4-star hotel is an 18th-century country house set in eight acres of grounds with south-facing views over the surrounding countryside. Leisure facilities include a heated swimming pool all-weather tennis courts. Gourmet meals and house specialities are served in the restaurant, converted from the old coach house.

Pousada de São Brás (tel: (089) 842305). About 12 miles (19.2km) north of Faro in the Moorish settlement of São Brás de Alportel, and open throughout the year, this small (29 rooms) *pousada* is situated on a hill, with beautiful views all round. An ideal base for exploring the east Algarve.

Restaurants

There are dozens of small restaurants in Faro itself and several bars and beach restaurants at Praia de Faro. In the town, **Cidade Velha**, Rua Domingos Guiero Largo da Sé (tel: (089) 27145), is highly recommended, as is **O Gargalo** at Largo Pé de la Cruz 30, offering excellent local food. Regional dishes served in a rustic ambience are the speciality of **Caracois**, Terreiro do Bispo 26–28, while **Dois Irmãos**, Largo do Terreiro do Bispo 18 (tel: (089) 23337), serves splendid fish dishes.

At Praia do Faro, **O Rogue** is the best restaurant on the beach for fresh fish and seafood rice dishes (tel: (089) 817868).

Shopping

The Rua de Santo António is a pedestrian precinct containing numerous shops beneath fine 18th-century houses.

◆
LAGOA

The pleasant inland town of Lagoa – not to be confused with the port town of Lagos, about 12 miles (19.2km) to the west – is the wine capital of the Algarve. Most of the house wine, both red and white, served in Algarve restaurants comes from here. Tours of the local wineries may be possible; check with the tourist office.

Lagoa is also an important agricultural market town, and a major centre for handicrafts.

Accommodation

The **Motel Alagoas**, Estrada Nacional 125 (tel: (082) 352243), has 22 rooms all with private facilities, as well as a swimming pool and discothèque.

Restaurants

For eating out try **Lotus**, Praça Marquês do Pombal 13, (tel: (082) 352098), or **Tia Rosa**, Urbanizaçâo Covas da Areia, Lole 21 (tel: (082) 352098) – both serve good local Portuguese food. The German-run **O Braseiro**, next to the market at Praça da República 15, enjoys an excellent reputation for good, wholesome food; also recommended is **O Casarão**, which serves typical Portuguese dishes grilled fish and meat, and has a delightful garden area.

◆◆◆
LAGOS

The popular tourist centre of Lagos is essentially a fishing port, set in a spacious bay, and like so many Algarve ports has a long history, having been first a Carthaginian, then a flourishing Roman settlement – it was called Lacobriga by the Romans – and finally an important Moorish town known as Zawaya. The Moors surrounded it with new walls which, however, did not prevent its conquest by Dom Afonso III of Portugal.

The town retains considerable stretches of its battlemented town walls, which afford excellent views over the roofs of the town and the magnificent wide harbour of Lagos bay.

Here, on 27 July 1415, a great Portuguese armada carrying 50,000 troops under Dom João, the Master of Avis, lay at anchor. It was *en route* for Ceuta, the great Arab stronghold on the African coast opposite Gibraltar, and whose subsequent capture marked the beginning of the great age of Portuguese discoveries.

The son of Dom João, the Infante Dom Henrique – better known as Henry the Navigator – won his spurs at the siege of Ceuta, and it was thanks to this remarkable man that before the century was out the Cape route to India had been found and both the Americas discovered. As Dom Henrique's captains pushed further south along the coast of Africa past Cape Bojador, they began bringing back negroes as slaves. The slave-market in Lagos – the first in Europe – can still be seen, standing close to the riverbank. Today, most of the activity in Lagos revolves around the Praça de Gil Eanes, containing the town hall and a modernistic statue of Dom Sebastião.

Along the northeast side of the

town is a wide seafront promenade, the Avenida dos Descobrimentos (Avenue of the Discoveries) which follows the right bank of the river to the Praça da República, a square surrounded by handsome buildings and containing a statue of Henry the Navigator erected in 1960 to commemorate the 500th anniversary of his death. Near the slave-market is Dom Henrique's palace, now a hospital, where you can still see the splendid Manueline window from which Dom Sebastião is said to have addressed his troops before setting out on his disastrous expedition. And round the corner stands the little chapel of Santo António.

The capital of the Algarve from 1576 to 1756, a large part of Lagos' architectural legacy was destroyed by the 1755 earthquake. Today, it combines the role of fishing and trading centre with that of one of the Algarve's most important tourist centres. The long featureless beach is not nearly as picturesque as others to the west, but nevertheless provides a good alternative because it offers an excellent range of watersports. Lagos itself is a friendly, lively town with much to interest the visitor. The shopping is good and there is a wide choice of bars and restaurants. The town is also well placed for excursions to both eastern and western parts of the Algarve. The coast around Lagos is magnificent, and it is worth hiring a boat to see the spectacular marine grottoes at Ponta de Piedade about 2 miles (3km) south of the town. Near here, the Praia de Dona Ana is a sandy beach reached by steep steps cut into the cliff and surrounded by strange rock formations.

Strange rock formations off Praia do Camilo, within walking distance of Lagos

THE ALGARVE

Chapels and Churches

Capela de São João (Chapel of St Joan)

Of medieval origin (possibly 8th/9th centuries), the chapel was restored in the 17th/18th centuries but is currently in a ruined state.

Igreja de Santa Maria (Church of St Mary)

On the north side of the Praça da República stands the church in which Henry the Navigator was originally buried. His remains were later transferred to Batalha Abbey. The church has a famous statue of São Gonçalo, the patron saint of Lagos, who is venerated by local fishermen because, it is said, he multiplies the shoals of tuna. Opposite the church is the Custom House, under the arcades of which the slave-market (Antigo Mercados de Escravos) used to be held, the slaves being tied to the massive iron posts (which remain).

Igreja de Santo António (Church of St Antony)

Associated with the army regiment formerly stationed in the city, the church contains on the altar a statue of the patron saint in field-officer uniform. The story is that he was appointed a major-general in the Portuguese army on full pay, which he drew through a proxy.

The 'golden chapel' of St Antony is considered a masterpiece. The walls of the chapel are decorated with 18th-century coloured *azulejos*; carved and gilded wood.

Open: Tuesday to Sunday, 09.00–12.30hrs and 14.00–17.00hrs.

Igreja de São Sebastião

Of harmonious and sober proportions, this church has Renaissance portals (16th-century), 17th- and 18th-century decorative tiles, and a statue of Our Lady of Glory taken from a wrecked ship.

Fortifications

On the southwest side of Lagos, skirting the waterfront close to Avenida dos Descobrimentos, are the remains of the massive old town walls constructed between the 14th and 16th centuries over others dating from previous centuries. In one of the walls there is a Manueline window from which, according to legend, King Sebastião attended an open-air mass before leaving for North Africa.

Overlooking the harbour is the picturesque Forte da Pau da Bandeira, with a museum (admission charge).

Museu Municipal (Municipal Museum of Lagos)

Housed in a building attached to the church of Santo António, this small museum contains a collection of religious art, ethnography and paintings, ship models, fishing nets, shells, books, pictures and a portable altar of St Antony.

Open: Tuesday to Sunday, 09.00–12.00hrs and 14.00–17.00hrs. Admission charge.

Useful Telephone Numbers

Emergency (tel: 115)
Hospital (tel: (082) 63034)
Police (tel: (082) 762930)
Breakdowns (tel: (082) 63183)
Railway station (tel: (082) 62987)

Tourist Information: Largo Marquês de Pombal (tel: (082) 763031).

Accommodation

Hotel de Lagos, Rua Nova da Aldeia (tel: (082) 769967): close to some of the Algarve's most beautiful stretches of coastline, this has been extensively refurbished. Facilities available include an indoor swimming pool and a jacuzzi, both of which are housed in a new wing. Each room is twin bedded with air-conditioning and balcony.
Hotel Golfinho, Praia Dona Ana (tel: (082) 769900). This spacious hotel stands on the edge of Lagos overlooking the Dona Ana Cove. Rooms are twin bedded with an *en suite* lavatory and shower plus a private balcony.
Hotel Meia Praia (tel: (082) 762001). A small, modern hotel about five minutes' walk from the beach in a somewhat isolated position, the Meia Praia offers a swimming pool with poolside bar, gardens, children's pool and playground, and tennis facilities.
Residência Casa de Sâo Gonçalo da Lagos in Rua Candido dos Reis (tel: (082) 762171) provides lodgings in a converted 18th-century stone mansion – a touch of the old Portugal in the back streets of Lagos.

Restaurants

The Alpendre, off the main square, has a good menu and a good wine list (tel: (082) 762705). Also recommended are **Dom Sebastião** (tel: (082) 762795) for shellfish in a rustic lively atmosphere, and **O Galeão** (tel: (082) 763909) for excellent traditional food.

The elegant town of Lagos retains stretches of medieval city wall

Shopping

A market is held in Lagos (by the bus station) on Saturday mornings.

LOULÉ

For those who appreciate popular architecture, the borough of Loulé is a real treasure-house. Alte and Salir are particularly beautiful, and Ameixal, Cumeada, Espragal, Benafrim, Querença and Bolinqueime are all examples of villages where it is possible to enjoy the sight of the picturesque architecture of the Algarve in its varied forms: in the *acoteias* or terraces that cover parts of the roofs; in the open terraces, covered with floor tiles, that are designed to take advantage of the rain waters; in the ceilings covered with reeds for good heat insulation; or in the chimneys where the taste for the decorative produces infinite varieties of shapes.

The date of the foundation of Loulé is unknown. What is known is that the Romans inhabited the area and that its castle is possibly of Arab origin. Loulé has been part of Portugal since 1249 when the Algarve was taken from the Moors, and it received its town charter shortly afterwards, in 1272. Today, it is among the places of the Algarve that are richest in handicraft products. Striking and attractive work in palm leaves and *esparto* (mats, handbags, baskets, bags, hats etc) are produced in Loulé and its neighbouring villages. In Loulé you will also find craftsmen producing copper articles, wax candles, brightly coloured harnesses, delicate wrought-iron work, picturesque clogs, cloth shoes and slippers, and pottery. Loulé has a notable spring carnival, usually held in the middle of February (prior to Lent), which lasts three days and winds up with a Battle of Flowers. The carnival is of relatively recent origin, the first having been held in 1906.

Sightseeing
Church of Nossa Senhora da Conceição
A simple exterior conceals an attractive 18th-century gilded, carved wooden altar.

Church of the Misericórdia
Formerly known as the Church of Nossa Senhora dos Pobres, this

The area around Loulé is noted for a wide variety of locally produced handicrafts

has an interesting radiated Manueline portal and a 17th-century painting in the sacristy.

Monastery of Graça
A ruined Gothic-style building from the 13th and 14th centuries, retaining some interesting features.

Arabic Castle and Museum
Captured from the Moors in 1249, the castle contains an interesting art collection. Good views from the towers.

Tourist Information: Edifício do Castelo (tel: (089) 763900).

Accommodation
Loulé does not have any large hotels, but the **Loulé Jardím** is a new 3-star hotel where the service is good, in Largo Manuel Arriaga 23 (tel: (089) 413095), or the **Residêncial Com Payo** at

Rua Antera Quental (tel: (089) 414422) is clean and comfortable.

Restaurants
O Avenida, Avenida José da Costa Mealha 13 (tel: (089) 62106), enjoys the reputation of being one of the best restaurants in town, but closed on Sundays.

Shopping
The pedestrianised Rua 5 de Outubro and the Rua da Barbaça near the tourist office are good places to shop.

◆◆◆
MONCHIQUE and CALDAS DE MONCHIQUE
There are two Monchiques – a pleasant little town of that name and its attractive next-door neighbour, known as Caldas de Monchique. The former has limited appeal to the visitor, although picturesquely situated, while the latter is a delightful place, idyllically set at 820 feet (250m) above sea level, sheltered from the wind in a valley of the Serra de Monchique.

It is an exceptionally neat and clean spa resort, whose waters were discovered by the Romans. They are thermal and said to be extremely effective in the treatment of skin diseases.

In 1495 Dom João II visited these springs in an attempt to cure his dropsy, but without effect: he died soon afterwards at Alvor, a village a few miles away. The heyday of Caldas de Monchique was towards the end of the 19th century when it was much visited by the Spanish bourgeoisie, and in comparatively recent years there was a somewhat derelict grandeur about the place, especially the little central square. However, restoration work has been continuing apace in recent times, with new restaurants and bars opening up to cater for the increasing number of tourists visiting the spa, especially on excursions from the main beach resorts in the Algarve.

Information on health cures can be obtained from Empresa Nacional do Tourismo, EP, Estabelecimento Monchique (tel: (082) 92205).

Monchique proper, 3 miles (4.8km) further on and nearly 1,000 feet (300m) higher, is a small town perched on the side of a hill overlooking an imposing valley of orchards and forests,

The famous Manueline doorway stands out against the white walls of the parish church in Monchique

and is famous for the Manueline
portal of the parish church. The
chancel is elegantly framed by a
semicircular arch of angels,
standing guard over the
Emperor's crown. Only the
chapel of the Santíssimo inside
survives from before the 1755
earthquake and the ornate
decoration suggests it may once
have been a chapel of the souls.
Further up the hillside you can
see the Church of the
Misericórdia. The building,
which was recently restored,
dates from the late 18th century,
and includes some fine period
carvings. The small, baroque-
style shrine of Senhor dos Passos
is also nearby and has two
belfries enclosing a statue which
is carried through the village
every year during Lent.

Accommodation

Estalagem Abrigo da Montanha,
Estrada da Fóia (tel: (082) 92131).
Halfway between Monchique and
the peak of Fóia, this *estalagem*,
or inn, commands fine views
over green hills, lush valleys and
the coastline. There is a main
building and a long tier of
separate apartments at the other
end of a pretty flower garden.
Basically a restaurant-with-rooms,
it is family-owned and enjoys an
excellent, well deserved
reputation for good value.
Pensão Mons Cius, Estrada da
Fóia (tel: (082) 92650). Privately
owned and managed, the Mons
Cius is a charming *estalagem* set
high in the hills. With only nine
rooms, furnished in traditional
country house style, the emphasis
is very much on personal service
and attention. The owner prides

Fóia
Anyone visiting Monchique by
car should also take the
opportunity of visiting Fóia,
which offers one of the best
views in Portugal. It is reached
by a clearly signposted road
that winds through eucalyptus
trees, which eventually give
way to heather and scrub. set at
an altitude of nearly 3,000 feet
(900m). Fóia is the summit of
the Serra Monchique, and is
marked by a concrete obelisk
and a forest of radio and
telecommunications aerials
standing on a windy moor.
If you choose a clear day for
your visit, you can see the
whole of the indented coastline
of the Barlavento from here,
with a panorama of the towns of
Lagos and Portimão and of the
wrinkled foothills stretching to
Cape St Vincent.
This is a popular stop for coach
tours, and there are a number
of stalls selling handicrafts –
needlework, knitted and
crocheted items, bags and
pottery – and a small shop sells
crafts and souvenirs.

---

himself on the high quality of his
cooking, and the *estalagem's*
restaurant has become one of the
Algarve's most fashionable
eating places. The hotel is an
ideal choice for a stylish and
comfortable holiday in a beautiful
setting well away from the
crowds, but in view of its location
a hire car is essential.
The Pensão Central in Caldas
de Monchique (tel: (082) 92203)
is worth consideration by
independent travellers on a
budget.

Beautiful terraced hills surround the picturesque little town of Monchique

Restaurants

There are a few reasonable places to eat in the town of Monchique, **A Charette** restaurant on Rua Dr Samora Gil (tel: (082) 92142) is very good. **Paraiso da Montanha**, at Estrada da Fóia (tel: (082) 92150), is one of several inexpensive restaurants in the area, and is noted for its regional cooking and chicken dishes, while the **Terezinha** (tel: (082) 92392), as its name suggests, has tables on an outdoor terrace (closed Mondays).

◆
MONTE GORDO

About 35 miles (56km) east of Faro, close to the Spanish border, Monte Gordo is not a typical Algarve resort, being dull and untidy. But it does have a superb sandy beach backed by a pine-forest rich with olive and citrus groves, making it a popular choice with sun-lovers, and in the last few years it has grown into quite a thriving and well equipped holiday resort. Safe bathing along this stretch of coast means that the resort is particularly suitable for those with children.

Apart from a bank, post office, souvenir and grocery shops, shopping here is limited, while nightlife revolves around the casino, which is situated on the beach. In addition to gaming tables there is generally some form of dancing available and a nightly floor show. Most of the hotels have discothèques on a regular basis, and there are also a few bars which tend to get very crowded in the height of the season. And like several other resorts in the Algarve, it is currently undergoing development, with major building works in progress.

THE ALGARVE

Excursions can be made from here along the Algarve coast to the west, as well as into Spain. A popular excursion is a full day trip to the Spanish city of Seville. For those who prefer to stay within the Algarve, there is a local bus service to Faro, which takes about an hour and a half. Sports facilities are readily available, with the larger hotels all offering some sort of water-based activity, usually windsurfing or waterskiing, in addition to a few land sports. Interest in the Monte Gordo bay area as a holiday resort is expected to be given a considerable boost after the recent opening of a bridge over the nearby River Guadiana, at Vila Real de Santo António, linking the Algarve with the Spanish mainland. Local tourism officials and hoteliers have responded by forming a consortium to supervise development. It has already approved the construction of three golf courses, a congress hall, horse-riding centre, a marina and other sports facilities, and further developments are expected.

Tourist Information: Avenida Marginal (tel: (081) 44495).

Accommodation
Hotel Alcazar, Rua de Ceuta (tel: (081) 42184). Widely considered Monte Gordo's best hotel, the 4-star Alcazar is within five minutes' walk from the beach and about ten minutes from the resort's centre.
Hotel Casablanca Inn (tel: (081) 42444-5): a small, Moorish-style hotel with indoor and outdoor swimming pools, a sun terrace, and a theme bar based on the movie *Casablanca*.
Hotel dos Navegadores, Rua Gonçalo Velho (tel: (081) 42589). This uninspiring-looking medium size hotel is within five minutes' walk of the beach and is about ten minutes from the resort's centre.
Hotel Vasco da Gama, Avenida Infante Dom Henrique (tel: (081) 44321). A large hotel on the beach close to the centre of Monte Gordo.

Restaurants
The two best restaurants in Monte Gordo are **Tapas** (try its seafood kebabs) on Rua Pero Vaz Caminha 24a (tel: (081) 41847), and **Stop 3**, serving good fish and seafood dishes, at Rua Gonçalo Velho 29 (tel: (081) 43672).

◆◆
OLHÃO
For years Olhão was celebrated for its white cube-shaped houses, much photographed and painted. Today, alas, 'progress' has all but destroyed the former charm and picturesqueness, with modern buildings having replaced many of the most appealing aspects of this small city, once reminiscent of a North African kasbah of dazzling white houses.
Today it is the Algarve's second largest town, with a population of just over 15,000. An attractive promenade now extends along the harbour and good bathing can be enjoyed on the offshore island of Armona.
The daily fish market held by the waterfront is reckoned to be one

of the best in the Algarve, and as a result several unsightly canning factories have sprung up on the outskirts of the town.

Nevertheless, the harbour area retains a certain charm and there are several open-air bars and restaurants.

At the centre of Olhão is the huge boulevard Avenida da República which leads through the heart of town. The main railway and bus stations lie just off this boulevard.

Beaches

Two of the most attractive beaches in the eastern Algarve are situated outside Olhão, on the islands of Armona and Culatra, both long, relatively peaceful stretches of white sand, offering limited facilities.

The islands can be reached by ferries from the pier every one and a half hours in summer (less frequent the rest of the year).

Sightseeing

Covered Markets

The large covered markets on the seafront are arguably the best and most colourful in the Algarve.

Fishermen's Quarter

This is an interesting area of narrow winding streets and low, square houses at the tops of which decorative bands, as opposed to the usual parapets, cover the roofs. Most of the houses were built in the 18th century and bear Moorish influence. In summer, delicious sardines are grilled on charcoal in doorways.

Igreja de Nossa Senhora do Rosário (Parish Church)

Located in the Praça da

Arab influences can be seen in Olhão's cube-shaped houses with their flat roof-top terraces

Restauração, this was built between 1681 and 1698 with donations from fishermen, and contains an interesting chancel and vault with frescos. From the tower there is a splendid view of the town.

To the rear of the church is a tiny chapel dedicated to Nossa Senhora dos Aflitos (Our Lady of the Suffering), a place where fishermen's wives come to pray for the safety of their men during stormy seas.

Open: Tuesday to Sunday 09.00–12.00hrs and 16.30–19.00hrs.

Ria Formosa Nature Reserve

The reserve encompasses the whole marshy area from Cacela Velha to Ancão, about 33 miles (55km) long, with an area of 42,000 acres (17,000 hectares). Ornithologists will delight in flamingos, geese, ducks, storks, royal terns and eagles and other birds resting here on their migration from northern Europe to Africa, and vice versa.

Tourist Information: Largo da Lagoa (tel: (089) 713936).

Accommodation

Surprisingly for its size Olhão lacks even one good hotel. The best it can offer is the **Hotel Riasol**, in Rua General Humberto Delgado 37, located near the bus and train stations (tel: (089) 705267).

Restaurants

Fish features prominently on the menus of most of the restaurants in Olhão. Among the best in town are the **Escondidinho**, in the centre, and **O Aquario** on Rua Dr João Lúcio.

OLHOS D'ÁGUA

Olhos d'Água derives its unusual name from a freshwater spring, or 'eye of water', which appears from one of the many rock formations which decorate the beautiful soft sand beach. Nestling between rocky promontories and pine-clad hills, Olhos d'Água was, until recently, yet another of the Algarve's small fishing villages little touched by events in the outside world. Now, its proximity to Albufeira and Praia da Oura have made it a popular choice among holiday-makers looking for a relatively peaceful holiday yet within easy reach of a wider range of attractions.

The new development has been confined to the outskirts of the village, and includes bigger supermarkets, more restaurants, and better connections with the surrounding resorts. In the early mornings housewives and tourists stand side-by-side buying fresh fish straight from the boats or fruit and vegetables from the market by the seafront.

PORTIMÃO

Approximately 37 miles (60km) from Faro Airport, and the peak of a triangle with Alvor and Praia da Rocha, Portimão is the Algarve's newest city, once of great importance as a fishing port, and still the centre of a fish-canning industry in decline. Nevertheless it is still one of the great Algarve experiences to sit at the cheap and cheerful dockside diners by the bridge at Portimão feasting on grilled sardines.

The 1755 earthquake destroyed a large part of Portimão and with it most of the vestiges of its past.

Sightseeing

Largo 1 Dezembro
This is a riverside garden that has become a cosmopolitan meeting place, with benches decorated with tiles illustrating important moments in Portugal's history.

Igreja Matriz (Parish Church)
Rebuilt after the earthquake, but with traces of the original construction, dating possibly from the 14th century, the church contains interesting 18th-century decorative tiles and a walnut retable, as well as a 16th-century statue of Saint Peter.
Open: daily 09.00–12.00hrs and 18.00–19.00hrs.

Tourist Information: Largo 1 de Dezembro (tel: (082) 23695).

As befits a deep-water port, there are many simple restaurants on the quayside by the bridge in Portimão serving fresh fish

Accommodation
Hotel Globo, Rua 5 de Ouctubro 26 (tel: (082) 416350). A 68-room hotel situated in a narrow street in the heart of Portimão.

Restaurants
O Gato, Quintinha 10 (tel: (082) 27674), is highly recommended for its excellent cuisine and pleasant ambience. **Casa Bica**, at Lota, is recommended for its fresh fish, and shellfish is a speciality of **Lucio's**, in Largo Francisco Mauricio (tel: (082) 24292).

Shopping
The main shopping street, Rua do Comércio, is closed to traffic and is good for general shopping, though there is little of

In one of Portimão's squares, seats are backed with tiles depicting scenes from Portuguese history

local interest. A weekly market is held in Portimão, behind the railway station on the first Monday of each month.

PRAIA DA LUZ

Towards the west, a little way from Lagos, is the attractive resort of Praia da Luz: a new village of charming whitewashed villas integrated with what little remains of the old village, and a sprinkling of restaurants, bars, and a discothèque. It is a place where the emphasis is on beach life and watersports.

The soft, sandy beach is popular with those who enjoy soaking up the sun, and the sheltered waters of the bay are excellent for the many watersports available, including windsurfing. There are also tennis courts available, and even microlight flying near by. Although a developing area, Luz

has created its own identity as one of the most peaceful areas along the coast and is a firm favourite with British families.

Accommodation

Luz Bay Club (tel: (082) 768962). Here, villas are offered for rental over short or long periods. The new village merges into the old so well that it seems part of it. Amenities offered include daily cleaning, three swimming pools, three restaurants, a bar, and good shops in the village.

Restaurants/Entertainment

Opposite the church, on the site of an old fortress, **La Forteleza** is pleasant but quite expensive. Other possibilities are the **Golfinho**, near the centre, and **La Granja**, half a mile (1km) to the north.

PRAIA DA OURA

Not so many years ago, when Albufeira was a small, slumbering fishing village, Praia

da Oura was its select residential neighbour, only a mile or so (2km) west along the coast..
Today it is a busy, modern tourist resort rivalling Albufeira for the quality of its restaurants, wide sandy beaches and practically non-stop nightlife.

At the crossroads, in the centre of the resort – known locally as Areias de São João – are the main supermarkets, banks and many bars. Close by is the newly completed bull ring with its modern shopping centre, Black Bull Pub and what is claimed to be the biggest discothèque in the Algarve. On Saturdays in the arena the spectacle of Portuguese bullfighting can be witnessed and, unlike in Spain, the bull is not killed in the ring (but usually afterwards, out of sight).

From the crossroads, the road to the beach is lined with restaurants, interspersed with shops and pavement cafés. Backed by rugged cliffs is the golden beach of Praia da Oura, where fishermen still mend their nets and drag their boats across the sand, oblivious to the inquisitive stares of the sun-worshippers around them. From here, cliff-top paths wind around small bays and inlets. Towards Olhos d'Água the beach of Santa Eulalia can be reached, and also the small hamlet of Balaia. Towards Albufeira, round a rocky headland, is the beautiful beach of Forte São João with several beach bars. Behind the beach, among several restaurants and bars, is one of the Algarve's best known and most popular discothèques, Kiss.

PRAIA DA ROCHA

Praia da Rocha is one of the most popular resorts in the Algarve thanks to its excellent beach – one of the best in Portugal – and its wide and varied selection of good hotels, restaurants and tourist facilities. It is a busy, bustling resort which is, sadly, still developing, with numerous new hotels under construction. The promenade and road are particularly busy and noisy, with bars, restaurants and shops.

The principal beach, about one and a quarter miles (2km) long and over 300 feet (100m) wide, lies below the town at the foot of the cliffs, and is equipped with the most modern facilities. The tree-shaded seafront promenade, a little way from the edge of the cliffs, extends from the Fortress of Santa Catarina above the west bank of the Rio Arade, to the Miradouro above the west end of the beach, from where there is a superb view of picturesque coastal scenery.

To the west of the resort are a succession of idyllic sandy bays separated one from another by projecting crags and reefs.

Tourist Information: Avenida Tomás Cabreira (tel: (082) 22290).

Fortress of Santa Catarina Built in the 16th century to defend Portimão, and containing a small chapel with a Gothic doorway, the fortress provides excellent sea views. There are café tables laid out on the old parade ground.

Accommodation

Hotel Algarve (tel: (082) 415001). A large modern, 5-star hotel above Praia da Rocha's excellent beach, with steps leading down. It has a large swimming pool set in a sun terrace area, poolside bar, gardens, children's pool, a quiet and relaxing atmosphere, spacious public areas, attractive dining room as well as poolside snacks, a discothèque, card room, gift shop and hairdresser's.

Hotel Bela Vista (tel: (082) 24055): this small, 4-star *residência* converted from an old mansion overlooks the beach in the centre of the resort, and is a splendid hotel that oozes character. The beautifully maintained public areas are equipped with comfortable old furnishings. The attractive dining room enjoys an outstanding reputation for its local and international cuisine.

Hotel da Rocha (tel: (082) 24081). It occupies a busy corner position which results in some traffic noise, but is popular because of its close proximity to the beach.

Hotel Jupiter (tel: (082) 415041). In the heart of Praia da Rocha on the corner of two busy roads, with the beach opposite. It has a small swimming pool with small sun terrace area, a poolside bar, comfortably furnished public areas, a large dining room, discothèque, card room, television, hairdressing salon and gift shop.

Hotel Oriental (tel: (082) 413000). This is one of Praia da Rocha's newest hotels, built on

Praia da Rocha: the Algarve's most famous beach, with its outcroppings of yellow and red sandstone rocks

the site of the old casino building, and is the first hotel along this coastline with an Arabesque look and feel.

Hotel Rochavau (tel: (082) 26111). About 20 minutes' walk from Praia da Rocha and more than five minutes from the sandy beach, the Rochavau is a highly recommended modern hotel offering a swimming pool with bar, spacious public areas and an attractive breakfast room.

Residencia Solar Penguin (tel: (082) 24308). A crumbling but characterful old *pensão* boasting the most perfect position on the beach – owned and managed by a charming English lady.

Restaurants/Entertainment

A Falésia is an attractive, first-floor restaurant with attentive service. The **Fortaleza Santa Catarina** is on the promenade in the old fort, and has a good menu.

◆
QUARTEIRA

Quarteira is not one of the Algarve's most attractive resorts. The extensive building work that has taken place here in recent years has both detracted from the former fishing village's modicum of charm and resulted in a flood of criticism from disenchanted holiday-makers annoyed by the constant noise of bulldozers and cement mixers. That said, it does have some 'plus' points, notably a long sandy beach, narrow in the main centre but widening towards the eastern tip. The main beach area is backed directly by a collection of large hotels which spill right down to the edge of the sand; the distance from beach to hotel in most cases is minimal, but this idyllic scene becomes distinctly noisy in high season. The beach shelves gently into the sea, thereby making it ideal for children, and the facilities – deckchairs, sun umbrellas, windbreak screens – are excellent. Small boats and pedalos are available for hourly hire and are inexpensive.

The resort has a wide selection of bars and restaurants along the beachfront as well as excellent shopping, with a colourful market once a week. The resort centre, alas, is uninspiring.

There is a good water slide park just outside the resort called Wet 'n' Wild.

Tourist Information: Avenida Infante Sagres (tel: (089) 312217).

Accommodation

Hotel Dom José (tel: (089) 302750): a popular hotel on Quarteira's promenade overlooking the sea and beach, close to many good restaurants and bars, with a friendly, lively atmosphere. There is a choice of restaurants, two bars, a small swimming pool, discothèque, television lounge, and shops. Golf, tennis and horse-riding can be enjoyed near by.

Hotel Quarteirasol (tel: (089) 302621): a medium-size modern hotel in the heart of Quarteira, within five minutes' walk of the beach, it has a small swimming pool and children's pool, garden area, poolside bar and an airy dining room.

Hotel Zodíaco (tel: (089) 389592): a good, small 2-star hotel with better-than-average facilities in a quieter part of

THE ALGARVE

Quarteira away from the much-publicised building work and dust. It is a five-minute walk to the Forte Novo beach and 15 minutes to the resort centre.

Restaurant
Alphonso's, near the Hotel Dom José, is one of the most highly rated restaurants in the resort.

Shopping
There is a market every Wednesday – one of the biggest in the Algarve.

QUINTA DO LAGO
This costly new resort complex lies hidden away in 1,700 acres (688ha) of prime pine forest land. Described by its developers as 'the lowest density leisure living area in Europe', it consists of top-class private holiday villas and apartments surrounded by excellent sporting and leisure facilities, as well as an exclusive hotel – the 5-star Hotel Quinta do Lago (see page 47).
Key attractions are a riding centre, considered one of the best-equipped in Portugal, and a 36-hole championship golf course. A fabulous beach (Praia do Anção) and the Ria Formosa Estuary – a haven for migratory birds – border the complex.

Accommodation
Hotel Quinta do Lago (tel: (089) 396666). This new 5-star hotel, part of the Orient Express Group, has already built up a reputation as one of the best hotels in the Algarve. A little isolated from the main resort, and two miles from Vale do Lobo, it offers a huge range of facilities that include several nine-hole golf courses, horse-riding facilities and a 29-acre (11.7ha) salt-water lagoon. It has several pools, and very attractive gardens. Fifteen minutes away is an excellent, unspoilt, long sandy beach, approached by a footbridge across the estuary.

SAGRES
Sagres is a small port 75 miles (120km) west of Faro on the southern side of Cape St Vincent, where Prince Henry the Navigator is said to have lived for 40 years in the Vila do Infante (City of the Prince), which included a fortress, a hospital, and a chapel. It is here he claimed to have founded his famous school of seamanship, or 'think-tank', bringing together the best astronomers and scientists; and it is here that the young Christopher Columbus learned his skills.
In the restored fortress you can

Forays into the Sea of Darkness
Europe's foremost geographers, astronomers and explorers brought their skills and experience to the famous school of navigation at Sagres Point, founded by Prince Henry the Navigator in about 1418. And from a nearby port Henry dispatched his caravels into the Mare Tenebros – the feared Sea of Darkness – in search of the world which he was convinced lay beyond. Thanks to Henry's enterprise, the Sea of Darkness eventually became the path to Portugal's place at the head of an empire which encompassed the world.

see the giant compass-dial – about 141 feet (43m) in diameter – laid out in stone which, it is claimed, helped him with his calculations; and the little chapel (not open) where he prayed. There is a tourist office (tel: (082) 64125) in part of the old buildings, as well as a youth hostel for budget travellers with a sense of history.

Francis Drake is to blame for the disappearance of the Vila do Infante, which was left half completed at the time of Henry's death in 1460; in 1587 Drake stormed the fortress and razed Vila do Infante to the ground. Within the fortress walls, a museum is currently under construction. From the battlements to the west of the fortress there is a superb view of Cape St Vincent across a blue crescent bay. The lighthouse of

The stone compass dial at Henry the Navigator's fortress and seamanship school in Sagres

St Vincent stands at the extremity of the cape.

The area in and around Sagres is not as lush as other parts of the Algarve, but is one of the few resorts on the coast which can still claim to be unspoilt and virtually unaffected by building work. It attracts travellers who long for grandiose horizons, spectacular sunsets and deep-sea fishing.

Accommodation
Hotel da Baleeira (tel: (082) 64212). A 3-star hotel close to Sagres, within five minutes' walk of the beach but in a somewhat uninteresting location. Because of its isolated position, car hire is recommended.

Orquidea Aparthotel (tel: (082) 64340). Within five minutes' walk of a stretch of sandy beach, this is a small, well maintained family-owned aparthotel in peaceful surroundings, with good views of the sea and harbour to the front and hills to the rear.

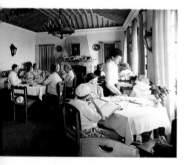

The Fortoleza do Beliche restaurant near Sagres

Pousada do Infante (tel: (082) 64222). A modern, purpose-built *pousada* on the most southwestern tip of Europe, with stunning views overlooking the cliffs near to Cape St Vincent.

Restaurants

The **Fortoleza do Beliche** (tel: (082) 64124), 3 miles (5km) southeast of town on the road to Cape St Vincent, offers excellent food in a converted fortress above the sea.

Shopping

Sagres is the centre for hand-knitted sweaters.

◆◆◆
SILVES

Beautifully located on a slight hill among peach, almond and orange trees, Silves was the capital city of the province of Al

Gharb during the Moorish occupation (AD714–1249), when it was known as Xelb, and in its heyday it was a larger, more powerful and more important city than Lisbon itself. It possessed opulent buildings, markets, gardens and orchards, and its inhabitants were renowned for their cultured manners, generosity, hospitality and intelligence. In those days Silves was a port trading in Algarve figs and timber from Monchique. Deep-sea vessels moored at the quays under the walls of its castle.

The silting up of the river destroyed Silves as a port, and the great earthquake of 1755 further contributed to its decline, although parts of the cathedral and of the battlements of its citadel survived this devastation.

Sightseeing

Castle

Above the town rears the massive Moorish castle with its imposing battlemented walls of red sandstone, heavily restored in 1940. A walk round the walls affords excellent views. In the courtyard are imposing vaulted cisterns, which still supply water to the town, and the ventilation shafts.
Open: 08.00–18.00hrs. Free.

Sé de Santa Maria (Cathedral)

Built in the 13th century but heavily restored after the 1755 earthquake, the cathedral contains the remains of a Moorish mosque behind its altar, a splendid doorway, and tombs of some of the Crusaders who helped to take the city.
Open: 09.00–19.00hrs. Free.

Cross of Portugal

Located on the Silves–Messines road, at the east end of the town, is a 16th-century stone lacework cross, over 9 feet (3m) high, with figures of Christ on the front and the Virgin on the back.

Municipal Archaeology Museum

This innovative museum focuses on a 12th century well and its contents – a wealth of Moorish ceramics, coins and jewellery. *Open*: 10.00–12.30hrs and 14.30–18.00hrs. Admission charge.

Barragem do Arade

A dam site set in the hills a short distance from Silves, complete with restaurant and picnic area. Boats are available for hire.

Shopping

A market is held on the third Monday of each month.

Tourist Information: Rua 25 de Abril 26-28 (tel: (082) 442255).

◆◆◆
TAVIRA

Tavira is often described – with some justification – as one of the most picturesque and interesting towns in the Algarve. It is pleasantly located near the mouth of the River Gilão, and although the port is now silted up and cut off from the sea by a huge spit of land, known as the Ilha de Tavira, the town is still important for tunny fishing. Until fairly recently, local fishermen strung great barriers of nets across the course of the migrating tuna, trapping them in the nets and spearing them. Tavira is divided into two by the River Gilão which flows through its centre and which is crossed by a seven-arch bridge, originally Roman and restored in

A walk around the red sandstone walls of Silves castle gives good views over the surrounding countryside

the 17th century. In the older part of the town narrow streets lead up from the main square, the Praça da República, to the ruined castle from which there are good views over the town. Formerly an Arab urban centre, Tavira was conquered by Dom Paio Peres Correia in 1242 in revenge for the massacre by the Moors of seven Christian knights. In 1266 it received a town charter, and prospered as an important port, being raised to the status of a city in 1504. However, a plague wiped out a large part of its population in 1645, while the 1755 earthquake almost destroyed the city. As a result of the subsequent silting up of the bar connecting it to the sea, it lost its economic importance, and for years stagnated, until the emergence of tourism.

Today, it remains one of the most unspoilt towns in the Algarve, with delightful small public gardens and fine churches. Buildings reflect their Renaissance façades in the still waters of the Gilão, and there is a delightful porcelain-blue tiled church in a narrow street lined with the intricately patterned tracery of lattice-work doors. Tavira is also a lively shopping centre, and has much to offer the visitor. Some of the liveliest activity takes place around the fruit and vegetable market by the long river esplanade, starting early in the morning.

Beaches

The best beaches are situated on the sand bar Ilha de Tavira, reached by ferry – buses linking Tavira with the ferry landing stage. The beaches here are surprisingly varied, offering on the one hand sheltered and safe family bathing in the Ilha facing inland, and a much wilder beach on the side facing outward which has developed into an unofficial, but generally accepted, nudist stretch (nude bathing is contrary to Portuguese law). There is another good beach near the fishing village of Fuzeta, and yet another about 2 miles (3km) out of town near the village of Santa Luzia.

Sightseeing

Castle

Only the walls remain of the castle, reconstructed by King Dinis in the 13th century.

Igreja da Misericórdia (Church of Our Lady of Mercy)

This is a splendid example of Renaissance art. Unfortunately, the church is only open for concerts but, from the outside, you can admire the very finely carved portal dating from the 1540s. The interior of the church has fine *azulejos* and gilded woodwork.

Igreja da Santa Maria do Castelo (Church of St Mary of the Castle)

This church was constructed on the site of a former mosque built in the 13th century and destroyed by the 1755 earthquake; some parts of the old construction can still be seen. A bold inscription recalls the memory of seven knights, members of the Order of St James on crusade to the Holy Land in the 13th century, who were murdered by the Moors. Dom Paio Peres Correia exacted revenge by attacking and eventually recapturing Tavira for the Portuguese. He has been honoured as a hero ever since. His tomb is a noteworthy feature of the chancel.

Igreja de São Sebastião (St Sebastian's Church)

This contains a small museum of paintings dedicated to the life and martyrdom of St Sebastian, as well as scenes from the life of Jesus and His Mother. Tavira has a further 35 churches including, on the other side of the river in the lower town, the Carmo and São Paulo, which both date from the 18th century.

Museum

A few miles out into the country, heading towards Santo Estevão, is an excellent museum, the Monte da Guerreira, known locally as Zezinho de Beja. One of the few valuable collections outside Lisbon, this museum is primarily a private collection of antique pottery, woodwork and paintings based in the owner's home.

Tourist Information: Praça da República (tel: (081) 22511).

Accommodation

Eurotel (tel: (081) 326041). The sprawling Eurotel is about one and a half miles (2km) out of town, and provides a good range of services and facilities. Although a considerable distance from a beach, it does have its own huge swimming pool and sunbathing terrace.
For accommodation in the town, you could try the simpler **Pensão Castelo**, Rua da Liberdade 4 (tel: (081) 23942), centrally located close to the main square and the tourist office, with views of the castle.

There are many beautifully decorated houses in Tavira, one of the Algarve's most attractive towns

Restaurants

Most of the restaurants and bars are clustered near the tree-filled gardens which line the riverside. Two of Tavira's best restaurants for fine local food are **O Casarão**, at Sitio Porta Nova 14 (tel: (081) 23151), and for grilled fish, **Três Palmeiras**, at Sitio Vale do Caranguejo (tel: (081) 22134). The **English Rose**, in Avenida Dom Matheus Teixeira d'Azavedo (tel: (081) 22247) serves chicken with clams among other specialities (evenings only).

Shopping

Tavira is renowned for its delicious caramel confectionery, widely available. A market is held the third Monday of each month.

THE ALGARVE

The River Gilão runs through Tavira with pretty houses on either bank

VALE DO LOBO

Vale do Lobo is widely regarded as one of Europe's finest purpose-built sporting resorts. Set among pine trees are 750 villas and apartments, built in a manner that borrows heavily from Moorish architecture. Unlike many other developments, it has been constructed and finished to high standards, with superior craftsmanship. The design has taken into account the natural lie of the land and complementary landscaping has made sure the whole place rests easy on the eye, even if it does fall short of the original concept to recreate a typical Portuguese village.

The resort is centred on the 18-hole championship golf course designed by Henry Cotton. There is also a huge 29-bay, twin-tier driving range where you can work on your swing without the pressure of competition. Other sports facilities include the Roger Taylor Tennis Centre with a number of all-weather courts.

Recently opened is Clube Barrington, a sports centre offering five squash courts, a gymnasium, one indoor and two outdoor pools, and snooker, pool, table tennis and games rooms. Other facilities include aerobics, jazz ballet and keep-fit classes, massage and relaxation rooms, saunas and a jacuzzi. The clubhouse is adjacent to the golf driving range which faces the new cricket ground.

The new centre complements the already extensive leisure facilities offered at Vale do Lobo, such as bowls, croquet, squash, and horse-riding. In all, there are 15 activities to enjoy by day, and some 12 restaurants and bars to try at night. Food ranges from hot and cold snacks to excellently prepared and presented international cuisine.

Local folk artists occasionally play live music in one of the resort's many bars during the summer, and one or two discothèques are organised in the evenings, including a particularly lively one most nights on the beach. The beach itself is particularly long and is reached through the main resort complex. Picturesque low red cliffs make a splendid backdrop and the beach facilities are excellent. Not surprisingly, the beach is very popular, and often quite crowded.

Accommodation

Hotel Dona Filipa (tel: (089) 394141). A member of the international Trusthouse Forte group, the Dona Filipa is one of Portugal's top resort hotels. Overlooking the sea, it is backed by the Vale do Lobo estate, and has lounges, two bars, and a first class restaurant. Guests at the hotel benefit from a 25 per cent reduction in green fees on the Vale do Lobo course, about ten minutes' walk away, and 50 per cent at Penina, while free golf is available to guests on the San Lorenzo course, some five minutes' drive away. For those not golfing, the beach is about 200 yards (182m) away, and the hotel has three tennis courts. Beside the pool, a bar and restaurant serve drinks, snacks and buffet lunches to guests.

Restaurants

The dining room of the **Dona Filipa** enjoys a good reputation, as do the restaurants **O Favo**, a bistro in Vale do Lobo Club Barrington serving expensive international cuisine, and the golf club restaurant.

◆

VILAMOURA

Vilamoura has Roman origins, as can be seen from the remains of Cerro da Vila, after which the resort was named, just across from the marina. Originally built by the Romans 2,000 years ago, the site was taken over first by the Visigoths, then by the Moors, before finally falling into disuse about five or six centuries ago. Now it is the Algarve's most luxurious and ambitious holiday development. Covering almost 4,000 acres (1,620ha), Vilamoura is said to be Europe's biggest ever private tourist undertaking, and has been built totally from scratch.

Already in operation are hotels, holiday villas, shops, boutiques, restaurants, bars, a casino, a nightclub and a host of facilities and amenities for sports and recreation, including a 1,000-berth marina (the largest in southern Europe), four 18-hole golf courses, over 50 tennis courts and lots of other sporting and leisure amenities. Of the four golf courses, the 18-hole par 72 Vilamoura Golf Club – Course I, in a pinewood setting, was designed by Frank Pennink and is regarded by many as one of the loveliest in Europe. There is also speedboating, sailing, swimming, fishing and skindiving; and even a private airstrip for those wealthy enough to have their own aircraft. All the larger hotels have their own sports facilities.

The marina is modern and well serviced, with a commercial centre complex containing a supermarket, shops, bank, travel agency, car rental offices, etc.

Other shops and facilities are to be found within the luxury hotels that form part of the development.

Beach

The beach is an enormous expanse of golden sand stretching east and west from the marina and arching gently down from its backdrop of lush pine trees into the blue Atlantic. Beach facilities, however, are surprisingly limited for so popular a destination, although most of the hotels are close by. Nightlife is confined to the hotels and villa complexes, where there are bars in abundance, and all the major hotels offer a variety of discothèques or live music entertainment. There is also a casino with live shows.

There is a small museum near the site which houses all the finds from recent archaeological excavations – everything from Roman lamps to Visigothic holiday money.

Accommodation

Hotel Atlantis (tel: (089) 389977). This is an excellent, modern 5-star hotel in a good position by the beach close to the two golf courses and approximately 5 miles (8km) from a riding school.

Hotel Dom Pedro Golf (tel: (089) 389650). A real golfers' hotel, the Dom Pedro is closely situated to the four Vilamoura courses, and to those at Vale do Lobo and Quinta do Lago,

Hotel Dom Pedro Marina, (tel: (089) 389802) destined to become as highly rated as the Dom Pedro Golf, this opulent and luxurious new addition to the family chain is situated in the Vilamoura marina, within walking distance of the town's waterfront with its range of bars and restaurants.

Ayamonte

Many visitors to Vila Real de Santo António take the opportunity to cross the river into Spain. Although there is a new road bridge about 3 miles (5km) north of the town, most visitors prefer to join the day-trippers and backpackers in the queues for passport control and the efficient and inexpensive ferries for the 15-minute crossing to Ayamonte. Ayamonte itself is an attractive little town about the same size as its Portuguese counterpart across the river. Although the road along the dockside is run-down and unappealing, just a street or two away from the river will bring you to delightful and bustling shop-lined streets and café tables set out under arcades. There is a central square in Ayamonte, corresponding to its counterpart across the river – with patterned mosaic pavement and a central monument. But citruses line the square in Vila Real while tall palms shade the square in Ayamonte.

Restaurants

The **Mayflower**, on the marina, is a pleasant place for watching the other half moor their yachts, while enjoying reasonably priced Portuguese and international fare (tel: (089) 314690). The swanky **Vilamoura Marinotel Grill** will cost you a lot more, but the view and the quality of the food (also Portuguese and international) is on a higher level in both senses (tel: (089) 389858). Two other

Despite its 20th-century holiday developments, parts of Vilamoura have their own charm

places to consider for good Portuguese cuisine are the **Bragança–Mar** (tel: (089) 315958) and the **Don Alfonso** (tel: (089) 312688).

VILA REAL DE SANTO ANTÓNIO

Vila Real De Santo António, by the Spanish border, is a showcase of 18th-century planning. The great Guadiana river separates it from its Spanish neighbour, although the new bridge across the river is stimulating an increased flow of traffic, and encouraging further interest in Vila Real de Santo António and neighbouring Portuguese resorts, especially Monte Gordo.

Vila Real has the only clear harbour of the Algarve, those of Tavira, Olhão and Faro being largely silted up, and that of Portimão, despite dredging, having trouble with a sand-bar. Vila Real also has the distinction of being a town originally built in five months – an early example of the kind of town planning common these days.

The place is the personal creation of the Marqués de Pombal, who was largely responsible for the reconstruction of Lisbon after the 1755 earthquake. He founded Vila Real de Santo António in 1774, partly as a feat of one-upmanship with neighbouring Spain, and partly to encourage sardine fishing. The first of these considerations led him to build Vila Real in sight of the Spanish town of Ayamonte, the second to evacuate the fishermen of Monte Gordo to the new town.

This he insisted on doing despite

A patterned mosaic pavement covers the whole of the central square in Vila Real

the fact that Monte Gordo was eminently more suited for drawing nets ashore, but when the locals protested the Marqués appointed a judiciary to decide which was the best spot for the new town. The judge chose Monte Gordo, Pombal responded by having him gaoled, and Vila Real was built where it is. The fishermen of Monte Gordo, for their part, immediately abandoned their neat new houses and went over to Spain in a body.

The streets of Vila Real run due north and south one way and due east and west the other, for the town is built to the same grid design as Pombal's other example of town planning, the Baixa quarter of Lisbon. In fact, all the stone windows and doorframes of the two-storey houses were shipped from Lisbon at huge expense, though a quarry from which they might have been cut for a fraction of the cost was later discovered a few miles from the town.

The heart of Vila Real is the handsome black and white paved square, which bears Pombal's name. It stands at the mouth of the river Guadiana, facing Ayamonte, and is bordered by exquisitely proportioned 18th-century houses and dominated by a narrow obelisk dedicated to Dom José.

A long and pleasant esplanade, the Avenida da República, lines the Portuguese side of the river and is a popular venue for afternoon and evening strolls. You can see across into Spain, and horse-drawn carriage rides are available during the summer months taking you past the shipyard and lighthouse at the edge of the coast. Carriage rides are also available to the castle at Castro Marim.

Among Vila Real's other attractions is the small Manuel Cabanas Museum, situated just off the main square, while the town is also the home of a major fish market, set up originally by Pombal himself in 1770s. Tunny fishing is carried out all along the Algarve coast throughout the summer months, but the peak season lasts from April to July when huge shoals make their way to the spawning banks a few hundred miles west of Gibraltar.

Tourist Information: Praça Marqués de Pombal (tel: (081) 44495).

Accommodation

Apolo (tel: (081) 44448). This is a newly built small hotel at the entrance to the town, with 42 rooms, all with bath. Breakfast is the only meal available.

Restaurants

Edmundo's (tel: (081) 44689), which is situated in the Avenida da República, enjoys an excellent reputation and also offers magnificent views across the river. Also popular are **Joaquim Gomes**, in Rua 5 de Outubro (tel: (081) 43285), and **Bonaca**, in Rua Duarte Pacheco. The **Caves do Guadiana**, Avenida da República 89 (tel: (081) 44498), overlooks the estuary and serves excellent food and house wine.

Shopping

Shops cater mostly for Spanish day-trippers wanting souvenirs.

Marquês de Pombol

The reign of the incompetent Dom José (1750–77) was dominated by his chief minister, the Marquês de Pombol. Appointed after the great earthquake of 1755, he embarked upon major reconstruction works throughout the country. He then set about to reform many aspects of Portuguese life, riding roughshod over his enemies – notably the Jesuits and the established aristocracy – in his zeal to stimulate capitalism, reduce foreign debt, abolish slavery, reform taxation, and erode the power and privilege of the Church and court. He dealt ruthlessly with all opposition, imprisoning and executing his enemies. Nevertheless, many of his reforms survived. When Maria I acceded to the throne, she banished Pombal to his estates.

LISBON (LISBOA) ✓

Lisbon, the capital of Portugal, lies on 20 low hills – not seven as popular tradition has it – at the estuary of the River Tagus (Rio Tejo), and is an attractive holiday destination in its own right as well as being a favourite excursion for those holidaying in the Algarve and other centres in southern Portugal.

The principal attractions of the city lie in the magnificent vistas from its many belvederes, its shady, tree-lined avenues and squares with decorated pavements, the freshness of its public gardens, its flower-filled balconies and patterned tiled walls, and its wealth of monuments, churches and museums.

The architectural heritage of the city bears witness to a brilliant historical past. The origins of Lisbon are shrouded in legend. Among its mythical founders are Elisha and Ulysses; it was occupied successively by Phoenicians, Carthaginians, Romans, Visigoths and Moors; and was finally conquered in 1147 by Portugal's first king, Afonso Henriques, with the aid of English Crusaders. But it was at the time of the Great Discoveries that Lisbon really came into its own, as capital of the Portuguese empire and world centre for trade in spices, jewels and gold. Examples of this fabulous wealth are to be seen in the Manueline architecture of Lisbon's churches, monasteries and palaces with their intricate stonework, maritime motifs and gilded woodwork.

The view of the centre and the Tagus is superb from the top of the castle

Centre of the city is the Rossio, a fine square with the National Theatre on the north side and surrounded by 18th-century houses, which the Marquês de Pombal, then Prime Minister, had built after the great earthquake of 1755. The streets leading off the square are lined with banks and excellent shops.

What to See

◆◆◆
CASTELO DE SÃO JORGE
Occupying a dominant position on one of Lisbon's highest hills stands one of the city's premier visitor attractions, the Castle of St

The climb is steep in Bairro Alto, one of the oldest parts of the city

> **Old Lisbon**
> Most visitors to Lisbon waste little time in seeking out two of the city's most atmospheric districts, Alfama and Bairro Alto.
> **Alfama** is Lisbon's oldest district, dating back more than a thousand years, and it is also the one which has kept true to its original form, remaining a labyrinth of twisting, narrow streets lined by houses with overhanging eaves, balustrades and lattice windows.
> **Bairro Alto** is one of the most densely populated districts in Lisbon, where palaces and noble houses stand side-by-side with humble dwellings, and where the streets and picturesque buildings vie with the many places of entertainment to be found here, including traditional *fado* houses. Bairro Alto is situated on top of one of Lisbon's hills, and can be reached by a novel form of transport – an elevator.

George. Dedicated to the saint since the 14th century, it has had a chequered and somewhat uncertain history, although it is known that the city was fortified by the Romans around 137BC and that both the Visigoths and the Moors adapted these fortifications to their varying needs. The Moors even surrounded the city with a protective wall, remains of which can still be seen.
In 1147 Lisbon and its castle were conquered by Afonso Henriques, and since then some of the most important events in Portuguese history have taken place within its walls. Vasco da Gama was received there after his discovery of the sea route to

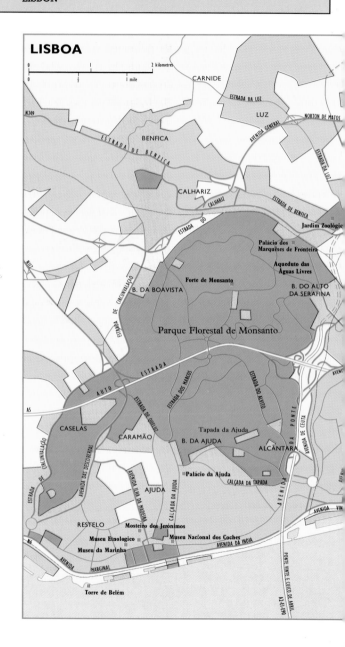

LISBOA

0   1   2 kilometres
0   ½   1 mile

CARNIDE

ESTRADA DA LUZ

N249

LUZ

NORTON DE MATOS

ESTRADA DE BENFICA

BENFICA

AVENIDA GENERAL

ESTRADA DA LUZ

CALHARIZ

CALHARIZ

ESTRADA DE BENFICA

ESTRADA DO

Jardim Zoológic

Palácio dos
Marquêses de Fronteira

Aqueduto das
Águas Livres

Forte de Monsanto

B. DA BOAVISTA

B. DO ALTO
DA SERAFINA

ESTRADA DE CIRCUNVALAÇÃO

NUT

Parque Florestal de Monsanto

ESTRADA

AUTO

A5

ESTRADA DOS MANGOS

ESTRADA DO AUTO

ESTRADA DE QUELUZ

CASELAS

CARAMÃO

Tapada da Ajuda

B. DA AJUDA

ALCÂNTARA

AVENIDA DE CEUTA

ESTRADA DE CIRCUNVALAÇÃO

AVENIDA DAS DESCOBERTAS

AVENIDA ILHA DA MADEIRA

Palácio da Ajuda

CALÇADA DA TAPADA

AJUDA

CALÇADA DA AJUDA

AVENIDA

PONTE DE CEUTA

AVENIDA VIN

ESTRADA DE

RESTELO

Mosteiro dos Jerónimos

Museu Etnologico

Museu Nacional dos Coches

AVENIDA DA INDIA

Museu da Marinha

AVENIDA VIN

N6

AVENIDA

MARGINAL

PONTE VINTE E CINCO DE ABRIL

A2-E1-E90

Torre de Belém

India; it served as a prison during the Spanish occupation (1580–1640); was very badly damaged by the great earthquake in 1755; and was used as a military barracks after the Napoleonic invasions.
The castle was restored in 1938. From the main courtyard one can admire one of the most panoramic views of the city, with the Tagus forming both background and frame.
Open: 09.00–17.00hrs. Admission free.

♦♦♦
SÉ (CATHEDRAL)
Largo da Sé
The cathedral is a fine example of Roman Gothic architecture, and well worth a visit. With its twin towers, it combines an elegance of form with medieval severity. Initially conceived as a fortified church, it still displays the formation of an ancient fortress. Of particular note are the 17th-century organ, the 13th-

Jerónimos Monastery

century cloister and the chapel in the nave and the 14th-century tombs of Lopo Fernandes Pacheco and his wife.
Closed for lunch: 12.00–14.30hrs.

♦
IGREJA DE SANTO ANTÓNIO DA SÉ
This is the Church of St Antony, the patron saint of Lisbon, who was born on this spot in 1191.

♦♦♦
MOSTEIRO DOS JERÓNIMOS (JERÓNIMOS MONASTERY)
Praça do Império, Belém
This was built on the site of the small Church of Santa Maria, founded by Prince Henry the Navigator on the orders of Dom Manuel I to commemorate the discovery of the trade route to India, and is an almost perfect blending of Portuguese Renaissance architecture and exuberant Manueline decoration. Its southern façade, parallel to

the river, is particularly impressive.

Much of the edifice was destroyed by the earthquake of 1755, but the splendid cloisters remain. The main portal is a masterpiece of chiselled stonework, while in the interior are extremely delicate pillars ornamented with motives of the Manueline period. These pillars support the vaults, one of which has an opening of 76 feet (25m). There are also several tombs of kings, and the tombs of two of the greatest figures of the Renaissance – Vasco da Gama and Luis de Camões.
Open: 10.00–17.00hrs (18.30hrs in summer).

◆◆◆
TORRE DE BELÉM
(TOWER OF BELÉM)
Avenida da India, Belém
Near the monastery, on the riverbank, this fabulous miniature fairytale castle is carved with openwork balconies, a loggia and turrets topped with domes. It was from here that the explorers' caravels set off into the unknown, and it houses a small museum to them.

Museums
Lisbon has an enormous range of really excellent museums. The following are among the most important and interesting to the international visitor. Most are open daily except Mondays and public holidays.

◆◆◆
PALÁCIO DA AJUDA (AJUDA PALACE)
Calçada da Ajuda, Belém
Sculpture, paintings and decorative art are housed here

The Torre de Belém is an impressive 16th-century defensive tower

in the private quarters of the kings and queens when it was a royal residence.
Open: 10.00–17.00hrs, closed Wednesday.

◆◆◆
MUSEU ARQUEOLÓGICO DO CARMO (ARCHAEOLOGICAL MUSEUM)
Largo do Carmo
This contains prehistoric, Phoenician, Roman, Visigothic and medieval works of art, as well as Roman, Arabic and Hebrew engravings and coins.
Open: 10.00–13.00hrs and 14.00–17.00hrs. (18.00hrs in summer).

◆◆◆
CALOUSTE GULBENKIAN MUSEU
Avenida de Berna
Surrounded by pleasant gardens which make it a veritable oasis in the centre of the city, this

museum houses Gulbenkian's private collection, later enriched by the Foundation which bears his name. Exhibits include Egyptian, Islamic, Greek and Roman art, paintings, furniture and decorative art, gold and silver, and *art nouveau* objects.
Open: 10.00–17.00hrs (14.00–19.30hrs Wednesdays and Saturdays in summer). Admission free at weekends.

◆◆
MUSEU DA CIDADE (CITY MUSEUM)
Palácio Pimenta, Campo Grande
Here the development of Lisbon from prehistoric times up to the First Republic (1910) is displayed by documents, iconography and engravings.
Open: 10.00–13.00hrs and 14.00–18.00hrs.

◆◆
MUSEU ETNOLOGICO (ETHNOLOGICAL MUSEUM)
Avenida da Ilha da Madeira, Belém
An ethnographic collection of great interest, covering various people of the world from all five continents.
Open: 10.00–12.30hrs and 14.00–17.00hrs.

◆◆◆
MUSEU MILITAR (MILITARY MUSEUM)
Largo dos Caminhos de Ferro, Alfama
Artillery and light armaments, models of battles, documentation, magnificent paintings and tiles are among the many splendid exhibits on display here.
Open: 10.00–16.00hrs (11.00–17.00hrs on Sundays).

◆◆◆
MUSEU NACIONAL DOS COCHES (COACH MUSEUM)
Praça Afonso de Alburquerque, Belém
Widely considered one of the best museums of its type in the world, with a fascinating collection of coaches from the 17th to 19th centuries together with harnesses, uniforms, documents, plus royal paintings of the Bragança dynasty.
Open: 10.00–13.00hrs and 14.30–17.30hrs (18.30hrs in summer).

◆◆◆
MUSEU NACIONAL DO TRAJE (COSTUME MUSEUM)
Parque do Monteiro-Mor
This museum contains examples of fabric from the 4th to the 19th centuries, clothing from the 14th to the 20th centuries, and traditional cloth-printing techniques. The 18th-century collection is particularly impressive. Temporary exhibitions are a feature.
Open: 10.00 (Sunday 11.00)–13.00hrs and 14.30–17.00hrs. Closed Monday.

◆◆
MUSEU NACIONAL DO AZULEJO (TILE MUSEUM)
Rua Madre de Deus 4B
A vast and well organised collection of ceramic tiles showing the development of this art form in Portugal.
Open: 10.00–12.30hrs and 14.00–17.00hrs.

◆◆
MUSEU DA MARINHA (NAVAL MUSEUM)
Praça do Império, Belém
Displays of naval maps, documents, models and boats,

navigational instruments, etc
with emphasis on the important
Age of Discoveries. The naval
aviation section is a 'must'.
Open: 10.00–17.00hrs.
Admission free Wednesdays.

◆◆
MUSEU DAS MARIONETAS
(PUPPET MUSEUM)
Largo Rodrigues de Freitas
An initiative of the São Lourenço
Puppet Theatre Company, this
museum contains typical
Portuguese and foreign
examples relating to this type of
theatrical production. An added
pleasure is a delightful puppet
theatre.
Open: Tuesday to Friday
10.00–13.00hrs and
15.00–18.00hrs.

Accommodation
Lisbon offers an extensive range
of accommodation, consistent

*Reasonably-priced trams run all
over Lisbon*

with its status as a major capital
city.

Expensive
Hotel Altis, Rua Castilho 11 (tel:
(01) 522496). About 15 minutes
by road from the airport and
within easy access of the city's
principal shopping area, the 5-
star Altis offers 307 well
appointed rooms.
Hotel Avenida Palace, Rua 1 de
Dezembro 123 (tel: (01) 3460151).
This delightful 5-star hotel, built
in 1894, is in the centre of Lisbon,
close to the Rossio. Facilities
include 100 rooms, two bars and
a well regarded restaurant.
Hotel Diplomático, Rua Castilho
74 (tel: (01) 3562041). This 4-star
hotel is well situated in Rua
Castilho, and offers 90 rooms
together with a restaurant, bar
and private car park.
Hotel Fénix, Praça Marqués de
Pombal 8 (tel: (01) 535121).
Centrally located, offers 114
rooms all with private facilities;
air-conditioning is a feature.

Hotel Flórida, Rua Duque de Palmela 32 (tel: (01) 576145). This 4-star hotel is near Marquês de Pombal Square, and has 108 rooms, all well appointed, an attractive cocktail bar, winter garden, gift shop and hairdressing salon.

Hotel Holiday Inn Crowne Plaza, Avenida M Craveiro Lopes 390 (tel: (01) 7935222): in the heart of the city, 3 miles (5km) from the airport and a few minutes from the Amoreiras complex, this is Lisbon's newest international-standard hotel.

Hotel Lisboa, Rua Barata Salgueiro 5 (tel: (01) 3554131): this newly opened hotel is situated in the heart of Lisbon, and offers 61 rooms and suites all with air-conditioning and direct dial telephone.

Hotel Lisboa Penta, Avenida dos Combatentes (tel: (01) 7264054). Situated about ten minutes from the heart of Lisbon, the Penta is a large, 4-star establishment with 588 air-conditioned rooms.

Hotel Lisboa Plaza, Travessa do Salitre 7 (tel: (01) 3463922). Just off the Avenida da Liberdade, this 93-room 4-star hotel has an attractive restaurant, 24-hour room service, and free car parking.

Hotel Lisboa Sheraton and Towers, Rua Latino Coelho 1 (tel: (01) 3563911). One of Portugal's most distinguished hotels, the 5-star, 386-room Sheraton is centrally located and has a wide range of facilities including a roof restaurant, coffee shop, choice of bars, health club and swimming pool, various shops, and a beauty parlour and men's hairdresser.

Hotel Lutécia, Avenida Frei Miguel Contreiras 52 (tel: (01) 897031): a rooftop bar and restaurant are among the features of this 4-star hotel in a modern part of Lisbon well served by public transport.

Hotel Ritz Inter-Continental, Rua Rodrigo da Fonseca 88 (tel: (01) 692020). Superbly located overlooking the Eduardo VII Park, the deluxe, 5-star Ritz has 290 rooms.

Mid-price Hotels

Hotel Eduardo VII, Avenida Fontes Pereira de Melo 5 (tel: (01) 530141). A rooftop restaurant overlooking the city is one of the popular features of this 121-room 3-star hotel.

Hotel Flamingo, Rua Castilho 41 (tel: (01) 532191). Well situated, the 3-star Flamingo offers 39 rooms, some air-conditioned, a bar, and a good restaurant.

Hotel Presidente, Rua Alexandre Herculano 13 (tel: (01) 539501). A centrally-located 3-star hotel with 59 air-conditioned rooms, all with private facilities, and a pleasant bar.

Hotel Mundial, Rua Dom Duarte 4 (tel: (01) 863101). In the heart of Lisbon, the 4-star Mundial has 146 rooms all with private facilities, and a private car park.

Pensions

For the budget traveller there is a good choice of pensions. The **Pensão Residência América**, Rua Tomás Ribeiro 47 (tel: (01) 3521177), **Residencial Castilho**, Rua Castilho 57–4 (tel: (01) 570882, and the **Pensão Residência Roma**, Travessa da Glória 22A (tel: (01) 3640557), are among the best.

Camping

The **Parque Florestal de
Monsanto** campsite in the
Florestal Monsanto Park (tel: (01)
704413) is considered one of the
best in Europe. Other campsites
to be found within a radius of 19
miles (30km) of Lisbon are at
Guincho and the **Costa de
Caparica**. You can use tents or
caravans.

Restaurants

Restaurants are classified into
four categories – luxury, 1st, 2nd
and 3rd class. The more humble
casas de pasto can also provide a
tasty meal. Naturally the price
varies according to the category,
but you will find the classification
shown outside, along with the
daily menu and respective
prices.
Lunch is served from midday
until 15.00hrs, and dinner from
19.30 to 22.00hrs. Should you
wish to dine later, *fado*
restaurants and pubs usually
remain open after midnight. The
restaurants listed cover a broad
spectrum in both style and price,

Lisbon is a centre for fado, *the
plaintive ballad unique to Portugal.
Some* fado *houses also provide folk
dancing for entertainment*

but all enjoy excellent
reputations.
Aviz, at Rua Serpa Pinto 12B (tel:
(01) 3428391), is one of Lisbon's
most elegant restaurants, with a
delightful period interior and
high quality cuisine. **Belcanto**, in
Largo de São Carlos (tel: (01)
3420607), is one of the city's
oldest and offers a choice of
dining areas. **Cervejaria
Trindade**, Rua Nova da Trindade
(tel: (01) 3423506), is not
expensive, but has enjoyed an
outstanding reputation for many
years, thanks to its atmosphere
and the emphasis on good
quality food, especially seafood.
Clara, one of Lisbon's top
restaurants, elegantly decorated
and noted for the high standards
of its cuisine, is at Campo dos
Mártires da Pátria 49 (tel: (01)
3557351). **Faz Figura** (tel: (01)
8868981) overlooks the River
Tagus, and is a delightful place,

stylishly furnished and decorated, with a verandah for *al fresco* eating in summer.

Pastry Shops

Lisbon is noted for its pastry shops. Among those worth seeking out are **Casa Suissa**, in Praca do Rossio, for home-made pastries and marvellous sponge cakes, and **Antiga Confeitaria de Belém**, in Rua de Belém, which was founded in 1837.

Bars, Cafés and Entertainment

Most visitors to Lisbon try to visit a *fado* house on at least one occasion. The *fado* is a sentimental song telling of days gone by, of tragedy and of unhappy love affairs.

There are numerous restaurants/bars where *fado* can be experienced. Most *fado* houses are in the Alfama and Bairro Alto quarters (neither recommended for walking alone after dark). Among the most celebrated are **Senhor Vinho**, in Rua do Meio à Lapa; and **A Severa** and **Lisboa à Noite**, both in Rua das Gáveas. *Fado* singing seldom starts before 23.00hrs and there is a minimum charge for food and drink.

Nightlife in Lisbon is not confined to restaurants or *fado* houses. All tastes are catered for – small bars, some extremely sophisticated with soft lights and sweet music; 'boites' (night clubs), with first class floor shows equal to the best in Europe; discothèques where the latest hits can be heard; and other musical clubs where jazz and Brazilian music are strongly featured. Most bars and discos are around Bairro Alto, Alcântara,

and Avenida 24 de Julio.

As for cafés, progress has not completely broken the traditional coffee drinking habits of the Portuguese. Three traditional cafés worth visiting are the **Brasileira**, in the Chiado; the **Martinho da Arcada**, in Terreiro do Paço; and the **Nicola** in the Rossio. These owe a great deal of their fame to the Portuguese intelligentsia who frequented them.

Shopping

Shopping in Lisbon is a delight, with an excellent variety of well made local handicrafts from which to choose as well as quality international goods. The main shopping district is the Rua Garrett, or 'Chiado'. Also fashionable are the low-lying streets running between the Rossio and the River Tagus.

Antiques: the most important streets selling antiques are Rua D Pedro V, near the belvedere of S Pedro de Alcântara, Rua de S Bento, near the parliament building, and Rue de S José, parallel to the Avenida da Liberdade. Here you will find furniture in pure Portuguese style, and also ceramics.

Capes: the traditional brown woollen cape worn by the people of the Alentejo has become so fashionable that it is now worn not only in the country but also in the city.

Ceramics: Portuguese pottery enjoys great prestige, and a wide variety is available in Lisbon's shops. Look out for the earthenware from Estremoz, figures from Barcelos, plates from Coimbra, Porches and Alcobaça, as well as artistic plates from Mafra.

Filigree Work: this typical Portuguese art with a strong Arab influence has great artistic value.

Lace and Embroidery: embroidery from Madeira and the Azores and lace from Viana do Castelo, Peniche and Felgueiras, are much sought after. Particularly attractive are tablecloths in woven linen and embroidered blouses.

Tiles: if you are fond of the traditional Portuguese tiles you will find an excellent choice. Viuva Lamengo in Largo do Intendente is worth a visit.

Fairs and Markets

Regularly on Tuesdays and Saturdays in Campo de Santa Clara, the Feira de Ladra offers a vast assortment of goods for sale. Visitors also enjoy ambling through Lisbon's bustling street markets, the most central of which is that in the Praça da Ribeira, where bargaining is still the order of the day.

Tourist Information: on arriving in Lisbon, whether at the airport, the Alcântara dock or at Santa Apolónia railway station, you will find tourist bureaux. Tourist services are also to be found in the Palácio Foz, in the Praça dos Restauradores (tel: (01) 3463643 or 3463658); Montra de Lisboa, shop 2016, Amoreiras Shopping Centre (tel: (01) 657486).

Useful Telephone Numbers
(area code 01):
Red Cross 783003
British Hospital 602020 day;
603785 night
Police 8149716
Traffic Police 8149716
Airport (arrivals and departures) 802060
Railways 876027, 877092
Taxis 7587229, 8155061

These impressive doors are in the Praça dos Restauradores

THE LISBON COAST

The Lisbon Coast is the name given to an area stretching along the Setúbal peninsula to the south of the River Tagus. Those who choose to holiday in this region have the best of several worlds: all the attractions of a lively, cosmopolitan city combined with magnificent beaches and unspoilt countryside a short drive away across the Tagus bridge. Major holiday centres in the region are the neighbouring coastal resorts of Estoril and Cascais, and the inland resort of Sintra. In addition, numerous other small towns, villages and resorts are well worth visiting.

Once part of the port of Lisbon's defence against pirates, Cascais, 20 miles (32km) from the capital, has grown from a small fishing port

◆◆◆
CASCAIS ✓

Since the late 1960s, when it was a tiny, unspoilt fishing port, Cascais has been developed to such an extent that it practically rivals neighbouring Estoril in size, with hotels, restaurants and souvenir shops on almost every square metre of land.

It is claimed that Cascais fishermen were the real discoverers of America. In 1482 Afonso Sanches sailed from Cascais and eventually reached America. Columbus, it is believed, learned of the feat and repeated the voyage.

As a simple fishing village Cascais formed part of the borough of Sintra from the time when Lisbon and the surrounding district were liberated from Moorish rule in 1147. Its own borough charter

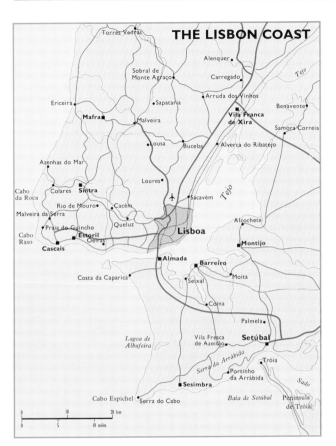

dates from 1364 in the reign of Dom Pedro I. The history of Cascais, however, is believed to go back much further, even as far as the Palaeolithic Age, judging from remains found in the town.

In addition to being a fishing village, Cascais has also been an important fortress, defending the entrance to Lisbon, and the village has seen many battles and many hostile fleets entering the Tagus. In 1640, after the restoration of Portuguese independence from Spanish rule, Cascais was surrounded by monasteries and splendid churches. Alas, the devastating earthquake of 1755 destroyed practically everything. The castle disappeared almost completely, one portal remaining as testimony to its former existence. Fortunately, the fortress and the governor's residence survived.

Since the end of the 19th century Cascais has been known as the Portuguese aristocracy's summer resort, though in recent years its development as a tourist resort has driven many of the noble families to seek out pastures new, quieter and less developed.

Sightseeing

Among the places of interest worth exploring are the former palace of the Counts of Guarda, with its splendid coloured tiles decorating the main entrance; the Church of Nossa Senhora da Assunção, located in front of the Parade Garden, which dates from the 17th century; and the Conde Castro Guimarães Museum, situated on the road leading out of the resort towards the Boca do Inferno. This delightful house was built at the beginning of the century and is now used as the town's museum and library. It contains a collection of paintings, porcelain, books, gold and silver work, archaeological remains, and furniture.

Accommodation

Hotel Albatroz, Rua Frederico Arouca 100 (tel: (01) 4832821): smart and exclusive, the Albatroz is built on the rocky cliffs and overlooks a pleasant sandy beach a minute's walk away. This former 19th-century villa was recently converted and extended to provide guests with beautifully furnished rooms in an attractive combination of traditional and modern styles. Although quiet and secluded, the shops and restaurants of Cascais are nearby.
Hotel Cidadela, Avenida 25 de

Abril (tel: (01) 4832921): an attractive, 4-star hotel, the Cidadela offers 130 rooms and apartments, each with its own balcony.
Estalagem Senhora da Guia, Estrado do Guincho (tel: (01) 4869239): once a private house, the quiet and peaceful Estalagem Senhora da Guia is about 3 miles (4.8km) from the centre of Cascais. With wonderful views of the sea, the hotel is furnished beautifully throughout in classical style, and has firmly established itself as one of the area's most fashionable hotels.
Solar Dom Carlos, Rua Latino Coelho 8 (tel: (01) 4868463): this charming *estalagem* was, many years ago, the weekend retreat of a king of Portugal. It is situated in a quiet part of Cascais yet only about five minutes' walk from the centre.

Restaurants/Entertainment

The **João Padeiro**, at Rua Visconde de Luz 12 (tel: (01) 4830232), is deservedly popular for its fish and seafood dishes – especially sole and lobster. Another excellent fish restaurant is **Beiramar**, Rua das Flores 6 (tel: (01) 4830152).
Of the many bars, **Casa do Largo**, Largo da Assunção 6, is one of the busiest and most atmospheric, while the **Van Gogo** discothèque, in Travessa da Alfarrobeia, is one of the most fashionable in the area.

ESTORIL

With its casino, beaches and swimming pools, cosmopolitan hotels, avenues decked with flowers and sumptuous villas, Estoril is a popular,

internationally famous resort, known as the Portuguese Riviera. The main resort area is near the Parque do Estoril, laid out in front of the casino, where purple-red bougainvillaea and stately palms catch the eye.

Well known hotels are situated on both sides of the park, while the lower end faces the esplanade and the beach.

The Estoril area is mainly a 20th-century development, although its curative waters have long been renowned, and St Antony's Convent was built as far back as 1527. But it was in the first half of this century that this pleasant hillside became an internationally acclaimed resort. Its gentle climate attracted writers such as Wells, Araquistan and Gómez de la Serna who took up residence there, and from all over the transitional Europe of the 1940s and 1950s, monarchs and statesmen sought refuge there: Humberto of Italy, King Juan of Spain, Admiral Horthy of

Despite the crowded beaches in high summer, Estoril has retained much of its charm

Hungary, and many others. Its casino has for many years been attracting celebrities. Standing on the site of the original, the new casino offers everything in the way of amusement – restaurants with floor-shows, shops, bars, a cinema, and exhibition galleries. The gaming room keeps to the traditional style, but as well as the sophisticated games of *roulette*, *baccarat* and *chemin-de-fer*, there are slot machines where visitors can try their luck.

Accommodation

Alvorada, Rua de Lisboa 3 (tel: (01) 2680070). This modern hotel is in the centre of Estoril opposite the casino. Rooms are spacious, and there are good views over the city from the roof terrace.
Hotel Atlântico, Estrada Marginal (tel: (01) 4680270):

overlooking the Atlantic, the 4-star Atlântico has 175 rooms all with private facilities, a restaurant, bar, billiards room, swimming pool, children's pool, and nightclub. Many rooms have wonderful sea-views.

Hotel Atlantis Sintra Estoril, inland at Alcabideche (tel: (01) 2690721). This excellent 187-room 4-star hotel has a wide range of facilities that include a swimming pool and tennis and volleyball courts.

Estalagem Belvedere, Rua Dr António Martins 8 (tel: (01) 4688556). This charming *estalagem* is well placed for Estoril and its beach and enjoys a fine reputation for hospitality. The hotel's rooms are simply but attractively furnished, and a courtyard garden provides a pleasant setting for a quiet drink. Other amenities include a swimming pool and a restaurant.

Grande Hotel, Avenida Sabóia (tel: (01) 4684609): the 4-star Grande enjoys views of the Atlantic, with 73 rooms and a restaurant and bar.

Lennox Country Club, Rua Eng Alvaro Pedro de Sousa 5 (tel: (01) 4680424). Centrally located in its own spacious grounds, this luxurious 4-star property is small and full of charm. Furnished with traditional good taste and style, it has a heated marble swimming pool and golf, tennis and horse-riding facilities. The restaurant enjoys a high reputation.

Hotel Lido, Rua do Alentejo 12 (tel: (01) 4684098). An attractive, 3-star hotel above the resort area, with a fine outlook across the pine trees to the sea. It has 62 rooms, a restaurant, cocktail bar, lounges, solarium, swimming

pool and a delightful terrace.

Hotel Palácio do Estoril, Parque do Estoril (tel: (01) 4680400). The 5-star Palácio is the most luxurious hotel in the resort, with a wealth of amenities including a thermal swimming pool set in spacious gardens. Nearby are seven clay tennis courts, three with floodlights.

Restaurants

A Choupana, in São João do Estoril (tel: (01) 2683099), is built on the edge of a cliff and specialises in seafood. There are many other excellent restaurants on the Avenida Biarritz.

Dom Pepe, in Parede (tel: (01) 2470636). Offers superb views combined with outstanding cuisine. Closed Mondays.

MAFRA

The town of Mafra's greatest claim to fame is the huge rectangular convent-palace which Dom João V had built in fulfilment of a vow made after seeking divine assistance in the production of an heir to the throne. Building started in 1717 and the work took 13 years, with 45,000 craftsmen employed on it at one stage. Expense was no object, and materials and ornaments were imported from the Netherlands, Belgium, France and Italy, as well as enormous quantities of marble from nearer home.

Tours of the impressive convent take in the church, hospital, infirmary and hospital kitchens, audience room, library, tower and dome.

Behind the palace lies a large park, entirely surrounded by a wall. In it roam deer, wild boar, lynx, wild cats, and all manner of wildlife.

◆◆
PALMELA

On the main road between Lisbon and Setúbal, in the heart of a rich farming district, the village of Palmela is dominated by a 12th-century castle on the foothills of the Arrábida mountains. In the castle João II (1481–95), forestalling a plot to overthrow him, summoned its ringleader, the Duke of Viseu, and personally stabbed him to death. Also implicated in the plot was the Bishop of Évora, who was locked in the dungeon where he died within a week. Excavation work is continuing near the castle following the uncovering of a Roman road.

Accommodation

The delightful **Pousada Palmela** (tel: (01) 2351226) is housed in part of the monastery of São Tiago which is inside the castle precincts. Ancient cloisters and monastic cells provide the setting for one of Portugal's best *pousadas*.

◆◆◆
QUELUZ

Queluz, nine miles (15km) from Lisbon, contains what is arguably the prettiest little rococo palace in the world, often likened to Versailles although on a much smaller scale. The palace was built between 1747 and 1794 by Dom Pedro III, husband of Queen Maria I, and its furnishings and decor reflect royal taste, including Florentine marble, Venetian chandeliers, Empire antiques and elegant furniture. The formal gardens were laid out in the 18th century.

Restaurant

The old kitchen of the palace is now a luxury restaurant, the **Cozinha Velha**, much favoured by discerning diners and for wedding receptions (tel: (01) 4350740).

◆◆◆
SESIMBRA ✓

Sesimbra, about 20 miles (31km) from Lisbon, was an important trade and fishing centre in the 15th and 16th centuries and played a great part in the Age of Discoveries. Today, it has all the charm of an old fishing harbour, with beaches sheltered by high cliffs and a coastline ideal for fishing and skindiving, sailing and other water sports. In the heart of the old quarter, steep streets lead down to the colourful fishermen's beach, bounded by a promenade. To the east of the quay lies another stretch of popular beach.

Of interest to the sightseer is Sesimbra Castle, originally a Moorish stronghold but rebuilt after the 1755 earthquake. Inside is an archaeological museum, while the tops of the castle walls offer splendid views of the bay and coastline.

Accommodation

Hotel do Mar, Rua General Humberto Delgado 10 (tel: (01) 2233326). A 4-star property offering 119 well appointed rooms, this has pleasant views from most rooms. There are two tennis courts.

THE LISBON COAST

◆◆
SETÚBAL

Busy, bustling Setúbal is sited at the mouth of the river Sado close to the last foothill of the Serra de Arrábida mountains. As well as being Portugal's third most important port after Lisbon and Oporto, deriving much of its income from fishing, it is also one of the country's oldest cities, with many fascinating reminders of its past.

The most interesting quarter for strolling in is the old part of the city between Praça Almirante Reis and the Church of Santa Maria, where narrow, cobbled streets are in sharp contrast to the wide thoroughfares of modern Setúbal.

Sightseeing

Castelo de São Filipe

The city's principal visitor attraction is the splendidly well preserved castle, built by the Spanish during their control of Portugal. There are panoramic views over Setúbal and the surroundings from the castle's ramparts.

Convento de Jesus
(Church of Jesus)

Built in the Manueline style in the 15th-century, this church houses in its cloister an interesting municipal museum containing a large collection of 15th- and 16th-century Portuguese paintings and 16th-century *azulejos*.

Accommodation

Hotel Esperança, Avenida Luísa Todi 220 (tel: (065) 52551). A 3-star hotel with 76 rooms, a bar and a nightclub.

Pousada de São Filipe (tel: (065) 523844). This lovely *pousada* has

Workaday fishing boats line the banks of the river Sado estuary, in the busy industrial town of Setúbal

The famous twisting pillars of many-coloured marble in the Church of Jesus, Setúbal

been created within the castle; it has 14 rooms (some in former dungeons) and a well regarded restaurant.

Restaurants

Rio Azul, Rua Plácido Stichini 1-5 (tel: (065) 522828), and **Galantinho**, Rua Occidental do Mercado 7-8 (tel: (065) 31924), both enjoy good reputations. The former specialises in seafood.

◆◆◆ SINTRA ✓

The town of Sintra is situated on the slopes of a range of hills about 15 miles (25km) northwest of Lisbon, and has been the inspiration of poets and writers throughout the centuries as well as the summer residence of Portuguese kings.

All around Sintra there are fairytale castles perched upon mountain tops, beautiful palaces and spectacular manor houses. Among these residences are parks and gardens which overlook forests and valleys, with magnificent views of the ocean beyond.

Sintra is a lively town full of shops, restaurants, cafés, palaces and museums. Old-style transport in horse-drawn carriages can be taken around the streets, and wonderful walks can be enjoyed among the spectacular scenery.

Sightseeing

Castle of the Moors

Constructed by the Moors in the 8th or 9th century, the castle is situated on two peaks of the Serra de Sintra, and from its walls there are magnificent views.

Open: daily 08.00hrs till dusk.

Pena Palace

This impressive palace was built by Dom Fernando II between 1840 and 1850 adjacent to the monastery which Dom Manuel I had built between 1503 and 1551. The palace contains a fine chapel with an alabaster retable and the cloisters of the old monastery.

The more modern part of the palace was designed by Baron Eschwege, and despite its pseudo-Gothic appearance dates from the 19th century. The view from the top of the dome, 1,590 feet (485m) above sea level, is stunning.

Open: daily except Mondays.

Royal Palace

This was once the summer

Looking out over Sintra's Royal Palace – one of several palaces in this glorious fairytale city

residence of the Portuguese monarchs. Constructed on the site of the old palace of the Moorish kings, it was mainly commissioned by Dom João I (1385–1433) who built the central part with the pointed arches, the Moorish windows, and the high conical chimneys. Dom Manuel I (1495–1521) added the right wing with the Manueline windows and the square tower facing the northwest.

Inside the palace are many fine tile panels and paintings, especially in the Arab Room, the Swans' Room, the Amorial Chamber, the Magpies' Room, and the Sirens' Room.
Open: daily except Wednesdays.

Accommodation

Hotel Palácio de Seteais, Avenida Barbosa do Bogage 8 (tel: (01) 9233200). One of the most impressive 5-star hotels in the whole of Portugal, this was originally a private residence and then a palace.

The formal gardens, for instance, can only be described as magnificent, the reception rooms and lounges elegant and beautiful, and the large, shady terrace a delight.

The cuisine also enjoys an outstanding reputation.

Hotel Tivoli Sintra, Praça da República (tel: (01) 9233505): the 4-star Tivoli is one of Sintra's newest hotels, with 75 air-conditioned rooms, all with *en suite* facilities, a panoramic restaurant, bars, a hairdresser, boutique and private garage.

Restaurants

Among the best in the area are the up-market **Galeria Real**, in São Pedro de Sintra, and **Quinta de Santo António**, in Rua Câmara Pestana.

THE ALENTEJO

North of the Algarve, and separated from it by a range of low hills, lies the vast Alentejo, which occupies almost a third of the total land area of Portugal. It is a region of delightful towns and villages, many of them popular excursions for visitors holidaying in the Algarve. Beja is the capital of the Lower Alentejo, and Portalegre the capital of the Upper Alentejo. It is a region which is not to any great extent geared up to international tourism as yet, but the warmth, friendliness and hospitality of the inhabitants – and the value for money encountered in the small hotels and restaurants – are remarkable. The region also contains a wealth of monuments, churches, palaces and old houses well worth exploring.

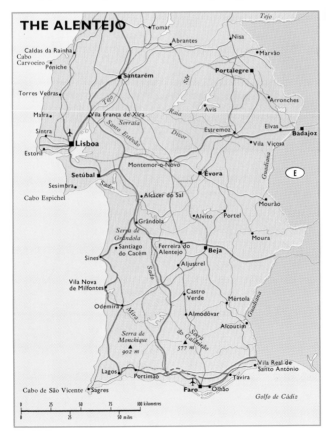

◆◆
ALCÁCER DO SAL

The small town of Alcácer do Sal
lies on one of the main routes
linking the Algarve and Lisbon. It
was once of considerable
importance. Known to the
Romans as Urbs Imperatoria
Salacia, it was subsequently a
strong Moorish fortress before
being taken by the Portuguese in

*Alcácer do Sal's impressive castle
fortress dates from the 12th century*

a siege in 1217 with the aid of a
contingent of Crusaders.
A ruined Moorish castle encloses
a Romanesque church; also
worth seeing is the small
archaeological museum housed
in the former Church of Espírito
Santo.

◆◆
BEJA

Beja is a pleasant town, and an
excellent stopping-off point on
the drive south from Lisbon to
the Algarve (or vice versa). It
was reputedly founded by Julius
Caesar, and for 240 years was
under Roman rule. Later, from
714–1162, it was ruled by the

Moors. It is a town of
whitewashed houses and
pleasing, cobbled streets.

Convento da Nossa Senhora da Conceição

It is believed that the celebrated
'Love Letters of a Portuguese
Nun' were written in this former
convent. The nun in question was
Maria Alcoforado, who lived
between 1640 and 1723, and
who became the lover of the
dashing Marquis of Chamily, a
colonel in the French Army, only
to be deserted by him. Her
passionate, pleading and
sentimental letters to him were
subsequently published in
France and later translated into
practically every European
language. The convent in which
she lived is now a museum
containing rare canvases, a Ming
ceramic bowl, church vessels
and vestments, as well as
archaeological remains from the
surrounding area.
Also of interest to the visitor are
the 13th-century castle with its
graceful keep and tower, and a
military museum.

Accommodation

Beja has no hotels, only *pensions*.
The best of these are the
Cristina at Rua de Mértola 71
(tel: (084) 23035), the **Santa
Bárbara** at Rua de Mértola 56
(tel: (084) 22028), and the
Coelho at Praça da República 15
(tel: (084) 25001).

◆◆
ELVAS

The town of Elvas is dominated
by an enormous and very
impressive aqueduct, paid for by
the town's inhabitants. It was
designed by Francisco de

Beja's 1467 Conceição Convent is now a museum with a fine collection

Arruda, architect of Lisbon's Belém Tower, was built on Roman foundations, measures four and a quarter miles (7km) in length and has 700 arches. The aqueduct was started in 1498 and took 50 years to reach the town walls and a further 74 years for water to flow from the attractive Misericórdia fountain. Elvas itself is a frontier town, facing Badajoz in Spain, and has been more strongly fortified perhaps than any other Portuguese town or city. Its well preserved 17th-century walls, complete with fortified gate, enclose an area measuring approximately 3,000 by 2,300 feet (1,000 by 700m), while the castle the Moors built in the 13th century is still there, as is the huge tower of homage built by Dom João in 1488.

The parish church was built between 1517 and 1537, although its tower dates from the 13th century. Of particular interest is a large organ which was built in 1762.

ESTREMOZ

If you appreciate simple but attractive pottery you will delight in the medieval town of Estremoz because it is famous for just that: round earthenware bottles, jugs, jars and panted figures for Christmas cribs. Estremoz is really two towns in one, since it comprises a tower, newer quarter as well as an older section, where a splendid castle keep stands at the summit of a hill. The views from here are stunning, while adjacent to the keep is a country museum housed in the old Hospício de Caridade and containing examples of pottery, furniture and church fittings. there is an excellent pottery workshop at the rear of the museum.

In the town's enormous central square is the town hall, which was formerly a convent, and the Misericórdia Church, with an

attractive Gothic cloister.
Of particular interest to the visitor
is the Museu dos Cristos
containing what is claimed to be
the world's largest collection of
images of the crucifixion – 1,400
of them at the last count. A good
day to visit Estremoz is Saturday,
when the weekly market is held
in the enormous town square.

Accommodation
Estremoz contains one of the
most attractive *pousadas* in the
whole of Portugal – the
impressive **Pousada da Rainha
Santa Isabel** (tel: (068) 22618;
reservations essential), located at
the top of the hill overlooking the
town. It enjoys a high reputation
for comfort and for excellent
cuisine.

◆◆◆
EVORA ✓

Évora is one of the most
enchanting towns in the whole of
southern Portugal. Built on a hill
that rises out of the Alentejo
plain, it is almost completely
surrounded by a perfectly
preserved 14th-century wall, and
contains many monuments
testifying to its 2,000 years of
history. There are many
picturesque whitewashed houses
and villas.
It was here that the dissident
Roman general Sertorius had a
base in 80BC, while Julius Caesar
conferred upon the town the title
of Liberaitas Julia. The beautiful
granite and marble Temple of
Diana, which is one of the town's
principal tourist attractions, was
built by another Roman Emperor,
possibly Hadrian. The temple is

generally acknowledged to be
one of the best Roman
monuments of its kind in
Portugal, although for many
years it was neglected and
allowed to fall into near-ruin. At
various periods Évora was the
residence of Portugal's
monarchs. João I gave his lovely
palace – today bearing the name
of the Dukes of Cadaval – to his
friend Martim Afonso de Melo,
who was Évora's mayor. Later it
was the residence of João III
(1521–57) and João V (1706–50).
Part of the palace of Dom Manuel
(1495–1521) is contained within
the public gardens.

Accommodation
Pousada dos Lóios (tel: (066)
24051) in a 15th-century former
monastery in the heart of the
town, this is a lovely
establishment with comfortable
rooms converted from the
monks' cells and a delightful
restaurant leading off the
cloisters.

Restaurants
Apart from the excellent
restaurant in the *pousada*, which
specialises in regional cuisine,
the owner-managed **Típico
Guião**, at Rua da República 81,
and **Fialho**, at Travessa do
Mascarenhas 16, are both very
good.

◆◆◆
MARVÃO ✓

The charming mountain-top town
of Marvão – from where there
are views to the Spanish border
– is one of the most beautiful
treasures of the Alentejo.
Everything, from the

The magnificent cathedral at Évora crowns the city skyline at night

whitewashed medieval walls to the twisting streets, is typical of the region, and its 13th-century castle walls remain virtually intact. Entered through medieval archways, the town has been of great military importance over the centuries.

Accommodation

Within the walls of Marvão's ancient castle – from which there are extensive views of the surrounding countryside – is the attractive **Pousada de Santa Maria** which, in addition to stylishly-appointed rooms, has an excellent restaurant (tel: (045) 93201). If the *pousada* is fully booked – as it usually is in the high season – you could try the

delightful **Estalagem Dom Dinis** in Corredour (tel: (045) 93236), which has been converted from a charming medieval house.

MOURA

The romantic legend of Moura Castle is what attracts most visitors to this little town, located about 32 miles (50km) from Beja. Built by the Moors against Christian attacks, it was considered impregnable. However, on learning that Salúquia, daughter of the local Moorish chief, was to marry a Moorish nobleman from a neighbouring castle, the Christians ambushed the bridegroom and his entourage on their way to the wedding, murdered them and dressed themselves in the dead men's clothes. They rode into the castle and so captured it. It is said that the heartbroken Salúquia jumped to her death from the top of the tower.

The old quarter of narrow streets and low-built houses retains the Moorish name of Mouraria, and is well worth exploring, as is the former Convento do Carmo, on the outskirts of the town. Inside the convent an inscription on one of the tombs states that its occupant died of laughing!

Tourist Information: Largo de Santa Clara (tel: (085) 22301).

PORTALEGRE

The name Portalegre means 'happy gateway', and although the promise is rather better than the reality the town does have some notable 17th- and 18th-century houses and other interesting monuments, palaces and mansions.

Particularly noteworthy is the twin-towered cathedral with its 18th-century façade, 17th-century organ and 16th-century retables; the 16th-century convent of St Bernard; and the even older convent of Santa Clara. Also of interest are the regional museum, containing carpets, paintings and sculptures, and the religious art museum.

Tourist Information: 25 Estrada de Santana (tel: (045) 21815).

VILA VIÇOSA

Vila Viçosa is a pleasant town set on an attractive hillside amid orange groves and containing the ruins of an enormous 14th-century castle.

Paço Ducal

The town's noteworthy tourist attraction is the Palace of the Dukes of Bragança, which was the home of the most famous of Portugal's noble families for more than 400 years.

Construction of the palace was begun by the fourth duke, Jaime, in 1501, and finished by his successors, one of whom is said to have murdered his wife on suspecting her of having an amorous liaison with a servant. It was here, too, that in 1638 Catherine of Bragança was born and where, two years later, her father succeeded to Portugal's throne as João IV.

The palace's interior, which is open to the public, contains many of the possessions of the last king of Portugal, who died in exile in England in 1932. On exhibit are tapestries, furniture, pictures and porcelain as well as Victorian and Edwardian items. There is also an interesting collection of coaches, carriages and arms.

Also of interest in the town are the Church of Agostinhos, rebuilt in the 17th century and containing the black and white marble tombs of the Dukes of Bragança; an interesting archaeological museum, housed in the ruins of the castle; and a religious art museum in the Church of Santa Cruz.

Tourist Information: Praça da República (tel: (068) 98305).

Accommodation

The delightful **Casa dos Arcos**, Praça Martim Afonso de Sousa 16 (tel: (068) 98518), is one of the most luxurious places to stay in the whole region.

PEACE AND QUIET

Wildlife and Countryside in Southern Portugal
by Paul Sterry

The wonderful climate of the Algarve, which lures holiday-makers from far afield, has also encouraged a great variety of wildlife and, indeed, many visitors come specifically to enjoy its spectacle of wild flowers, birds and insects. Influenced by the Mediterranean and the Atlantic, the Algarve is a meeting place for species with both eastern and western distributions and the range of wildlife is astonishing. Another secret of the richness of the Algarve's wildlife lies in the variety of habitats within the region. Cliffs, sand dunes and marshes are found along the coast – although tourist developments are placing increasing pressure on them – while inland, the rolling, scrub-covered landscape and groves of olive and almond eventually give way to hills in the north of the region.

Although all these different habitats can be seen in a single day's drive, each merits

Storks are a common sight in the Alentejo: these are nesting in Alcácer do Sal

at least a full day's exploration on its own, and visitors are sure to find that a week or two is not enough to do the Algarve justice.

Freshwater in the Algarve

Many of the freshwater habitats in the Algarve have been so radically altered in recent times that they have either lost much of their wildlife interest or disappeared completely. However, here and there, areas of freshwater remain and act as magnets for the animals of the surrounding land.

Pride of place must go to the Ludo marshes, which lie near the perimeter of Faro airport. Now enjoying a degree of protection and guarded by savage, chained dogs, this vast area of saltpans, lagoons and reedbeds is internationally famous and, although access without prior permission is limited, a wealth of birdlife can be seen from its boundaries.

From the banks of the saltpans (which now support colourful flowers such as tongue orchids) views of waders, including black-winged stilt, avocet, little stint and ruff, can be had as they probe the mud for food.

Overhead, swifts and swallows hunt for insects and are sometimes joined by collared pratincoles which, despite their swallow-like appearance, are really waders. Little egrets wade in the deeper water, sometimes with spoonbills and white storks, in the winter months.

Bushes and reedbeds are alive with bird song in the spring, with Cetti's, fan-tailed and reed warblers sometimes singing from exposed perches. Despite their greater size, purple herons are more difficult to see, since they lurk in the cover of the reeds, and the little bitterns are equally shy and retiring.

Many former marshes in the Algarve have now been reclaimed, but those that are used as rice paddies, as around Lagos, are sometimes good for birdwatching. Small patches of reed often remain and serve as a refuge for shy species, while cattle and little egrets, black-winged stilts and little stints often congregate after the rice has been harvested.

Reservoirs built in the hills further north, such as the Barragem da Bravura, can sometimes be rather disappointing for the birdwatcher. Lesser black-backed gulls, swallows and, in winter, crag martins are often the only species visible. However, the colourful *Cistus* scrub which

Purple Gallinules

The Ludo marshes are perhaps most famous for their colony of purple gallinules, which are also rather secretive birds. Dawn and dusk are the best times to see them, as they emerge from cover to feed along the muddy margins. They are worth waiting for, since they look quite unlike any other European bird. Huge red feet at the end of long red legs, gaudy, bluish-purple plumage and an immense red bill rather like a parrot's make them contenders for denizens of some steamy primeval jungle rather than a Portuguese swamp.

often surrounds the reservoirs may harbour subalpine and Sardinian warblers.

The Coastline

The Algarve possesses a delightful range of coastal scenery, from the dramatic and inspiring cliffs of Cape St Vincent and Sagres in the west to sand dunes and coastal lagoons around Faro. Although marred in places by tourist development, there are still many areas which are comparatively unspoilt and offer rich rewards for visiting naturalists.

Not all the cliffs are as wild and rugged as Cape St Vincent, but where sandstone forms the bedrock the eroded formations often create beautiful shapes and hues. At Ponta da Piedade, south of Lagos, for example, natural pillars, stacks and arches have formed through centuries of erosion by sea and wind. Although breeding seabirds are

Ponta da Piedade is a good place to watch sea birds on their way north

disappointingly few, some of the offshore stacks have large colonies of cattle egrets, whose relatives, the little egrets, sometimes come for a visit. Headlands and promontories such as Ponta da Piedade are also good spots to watch the passage of seabirds such as Cory's shearwaters, which fly by during periods of onshore winds. Winds from the south in spring also encourage the migration of birds from Africa to Europe; and parties of bee-eaters fly in from the sea in March and April to join groups of common, pallid and alpine swifts.

The rocky coastlines also have a large range of plants, which are at their most colourful in spring. Many different species of rockrose grow here and produce crinkly, white, pink or purple flowers which are much

PEACE AND QUIET

The strange saltmarsh broomrape grows in profusion along the Algarve coast

favoured by butterflies and other insects. Species of heather, broom and the colourful catchfly *Silene colorata* also add colour, and often thrive where bushes of joint pine or stone pine woodlands provide a degree of shade. Serins and Sardinian warblers sing from their boughs, while the carpet of fallen leaves in undisturbed woodlands may support nesting red-necked nightjars, almost impossible to spot, thanks to their cryptically marked plumage.

Nearer to Faro, visitors will find areas of sandy beaches, sand dunes and saltmarsh. The shoreline is often littered with the remains of heart urchins, which live buried in the sand below the low tide line; while, above the strandline, sea heath and sea knotgrass grow in prostrate form. Sea spurge and sea stocks are more bushy in appearance, but most extraordinary of all is the parasitic saltmarsh broomrape *Cistanche phelypea*, which produces yellow flower spikes out of bare sand, close to its host plants, seablite and sea purslane.

The Alvor Estuary

To the south of the town of Mexilhoeira Grande lies the last unspoilt estuary in the Algarve. The estuary of the Alvor river is rich in wildlife, so much so that not only does it support large populations of birds, but its fish and shellfish are the basis for the whole economy of the local community.

As the river winds its way towards the sea, vast mudflats and sand banks are formed and stretch over huge areas at low tide. Immense numbers of marine worms and shellfish, such as tellins and cockles, thrive in these conditions, and armies of fiddler crabs can be seen at low tide, brandishing their brightly coloured pincers. Not surprisingly, wading birds such as whimbrel, godwits, redshank and dunlin stop off to feed while on migration, many of them remaining throughout the winter. Little egrets, as well as the occasional grey heron and white stork, stride elegantly through the channels at low tide, often accompanied by scavenging black-headed and lesser black-backed gulls. Study the roosting gulls closely and you may spot a Caspian tern among them. From

October until April a few of these large birds can be seen regularly here and are easily recognised by their large, orange bills. During the summer months diminutive little terns replace them, nesting on the landward side of the seawall.

To the east of the estuary, a series of old saltpans provides a wonderful habitat for nesting birds. Large patches of sea heath and buttonweed sometimes harbour quail in the spring, while the equally secretive stone curlew is resident throughout the year. Huge, yellow eyes reveal its nocturnal lifestyle; but even at dusk, when it becomes active, it creeps among the vegetation and is very difficult for the birdwatcher to spot.

Short-toed larks, fan-tailed warblers and Iberian yellow wagtails are much more conspicuous. Ridges and banks around the wetter saltpans are ideal spots for the nests of black-winged stilts, birds with extraordinarily long, red legs which enable them to wade through the deepest pools. The length of the legs is, however, a real drawback when it comes to settling on the nest, and sitting still they look very peculiar indeed.

Not surprisingly, an area such as the Alvor is under constant threat from development, which could wipe out its wildlife interest and role in the fishing economy almost overnight. Fortunately, the community at nearby A Rocha has established a field study centre, which is developing both local and national interest in the area and helping to safeguard its future.

The Flowers of Cape St Vincent

At the southwest tip of Portugal lie the headlands of Sagres and Cape St Vincent, windswept outcrops which are pounded by the full force of the Atlantic. The cliffs are sheer and the headlands themselves are scoured by gales, but, despite this, an amazing array of plants greets the eye. Because of the stunting effect of the wind and grazing animals, the plants are often low-growing, but they more than make up for this with the dazzling variety of flowers on show between February and June.

The unique climate and the comparative isolation of the area mean that many of the plants found here are endemic to the Algarve. Some are restricted to the Cape St Vincent area itself: squill, knapweed and thrift all have endemic forms.

One of the dominant flowering groups of Cape St Vincent and, indeed, of unspoilt parts of the Algarve coast in general, are the cistuses: colourful members of the rockrose family. In order to combat the threat of drought, the leaves have evolved a variety of strategies in different species: some have waxy leaf surfaces, while others have inrolled margins, or a hairy undersurface. The endemic *Cistus palhinhae*, with its shiny leaves, grows low to the ground and produces crinkly, white flowers which are rather similar to the gum cistus *C ladanifer*. This latter plant forms more of a bush, and its sticky leaves contribute to the characteristic aroma of the region. Several other species are

PEACE AND QUIET

Many attractive flowering plants can be seen around Cape St Vincent, notably forms of thrift (above) and cistuses (below). Some plants here grow nowhere else

common, including sage-leaved (*C salvifolius*) and grey-leaved (*C albidus*) cistus, the latter with beautiful magenta flowers.
A careful search between the clumps of cistus, juniper and Hottentot fig will reveal patches of rosemary and thyme, adding to the fragrance of the spring air.

Many of the plants grow in compact form to resist desiccation, and the milk vetch *Astragalus massiliensis*, which has creamy flowers in April and May, forms compact 'hedgehog' clumps, so-called because of their protective spines. Close to the cliff edge, clumps of the endemic thrift *Armeria pungens* grow and produce tall heads of pink flowers in April and early May, alongside the striking yellow umbellifer *Cachrys cicula*.

The Birds of Cape St Vincent
With its position as the 'Land's End' of Europe, Cape St Vincent is of immense importance to migrating birds. Unwilling to fly directly over the headland, sea birds stream past the cliffs in huge numbers in spring and autumn, while land birds use it as a staging post between Europe and Africa, and almost any species found in western Europe may turn up.
Among the land birds, birds of prey are the least inclined to cross large expanses of water, as

they cannot get the 'lift' they need to glide and circle. However, although most of Iberia's raptors use the narrow Straits of Gibraltar as the gateway to western Europe, Cape St Vincent regularly attracts migrant ospreys, booted eagles, short-toed eagles and the occasional black kite. On reaching land, they soon radiate out across the fields and are quickly lost to sight.

March and April see the arrival of migrant songbirds, which often feed alongside resident black redstarts and crested larks. Parties of common, pallid and Alpine swifts use updraughts from the cliffs to race through the air in search of insects; and small groups of bee-eaters arrive soon afterwards. Some stay to breed a short way inland, where they excavate burrows in sandy banks and roadside verges. A similar range of species is found during autumn migration, but, perhaps surprisingly, Alpine accentors are then a regular feature, small parties remaining throughout the winter months on the cliff edge.

Sea bird passage past the Cape can also be spectacular. Gannets stream by in their hundreds, sometimes harried by great skuas, while keen-eyed observers may see petrels dancing between the waves below. Since the cliffs are so high, it takes skill and experience to distinguish storm petrels from Wilson's petrels, which can both be seen here, but observers should have less difficulty with their larger relatives, the shearwaters. Manx and Cory's shearwaters share the same stiff-winged flight pattern, but the larger size of Cory's is immediately obvious.

Travelling north and inland from the Cape towards Vila do Bispo, the visitor passes through wide-open fields of marigolds and tassel hyacinth. These regions are the haunt of stone curlews and little bustards, the numbers of resident birds being swollen in winter by visitors from further north, and by the occasional crane or great bustard.

The Hills of the Northern Algarve

As you head inland from the coast of the Algarve, the land rises gently to a range of hills that form the boundary with the Alentejo region to the north. Although not especially high or dramatic, these hills provide an interesting contrast to the landscape and wildlife of the coast and, often, a welcome break from the searing heat of the southern coastal areas in the summer months.

The drive inland takes you through landscapes which have been largely cleared of their natural vegetation. Groves of cork oak are still encouraged, however, and scrubby habitat still persists, full of *Cistus*, broom, birthwort, two-leaved squill and several species of orchid. Look also for the strawberry tree, whose fruits gave it its name and which are made into a local brandy called *medronho*. On the ground below, crickets sing from their burrow entrances and colourful swallowtail, two-tailed pashas and Cleopatra butterflies search for nectar.

PEACE AND QUIET

Patches of scrub have nightingales and Dartford warblers, and larger trees may sometimes host firecrest or crested tit. Plantations of eucalyptus are becoming an increasingly

The azure-winged magpie is a bright sight away from the coast of the Algarve

common sight across the hillsides. While this alien species does little to encourage most native animals, it is, however, favoured by one of Portugal's most colourful species, the azure-winged magpie, which often nests in small colonies close to the road. This bird has a most unusual worldwide distribution, for, apart from the Iberian Peninsula, it is only found in the Far East.

Serra de Monchique is easily accessible and one of the most interesting parts of the hilly regions. Shortly before reaching the highest point, the road passes through the spa of Caldas de Monchique, a charming spot to stop for refreshments. A short walk to the spa source will reveal a small colony of Bosca's newt, which has an extremely restricted distribution in Europe. Monchique itself consists of two peaks: Picota and the slightly higher Fóia. The high rainfall, acid soils and land clearance have led to a rather restricted flora, but what does occur attracts botanists.

The squill *Scilla monophyllos* and crocus *Romulea bulbocodium* are common, and in wet flushes, delicate trails of coral necklace can be found. Of greater interest to serious botanists, however, is a comparatively insignificant but, nevertheless, intriguing fern called sand quillwort, which looks more like a miniature tussock of grass than a true fern.

The Alentejo

Lying to the north of the range of hills which forms the northern boundary of the Algarve, the Alentejo is a region of vast plains and rolling hills. The temperatures are excessively hot in the summer and the rainfall is minimal, so, not surprisingly, the plants and animals of the Alentejo contrast markedly with those of the Algarve. Although much of the land is now given over to agriculture, the region's most important species still persist in some numbers.

Cranes winter in the region, so look carefully at any groups of large birds.

The arid conditions of the

Bustards of the Alentejo
Fields of yellow lupin, sage and lavender are a colourful sight in spring, but scan the fields from a distance and you may see heads appearing above flowers. These belong to little bustards, resident and secretive birds of central Iberia. Always wary of man, the bustards are at their most confident in spring, when the males advertise their territories at display grounds early in the morning.

Despite centuries of persecution, great bustards are also still found in the Alentejo. Although they are Europe's largest flying birds they are also among the shyest, preferring the vast, open arable fields so characteristic of the region. As with their smaller relatives, spring is the best time to see them, when males perform extraordinary displays with inflated throat pouches and ruffled neck, wing and tail feathers. During the winter months, the bustards often form large flocks which, in flight, are comparatively easy to spot.

the black-winged kite, one of the Alentejo's rarest birds. This elegant bird of prey is easily distinguished by its black, grey and white plumage from the far commoner Montagu's harrier,

The shy great bustard can still be seen in the Alentejo

which nests on the ground. Although dry and dusty, towns and villages in the Alentejo still have many interesting birds. Hoopoes and crested larks often feed beside the road, while churches and, more especially, ruined castles sometimes have black wheatears and colonies of lesser kestrels.

Spring Flowers
From February until June, the Algarve comes alive with colourful flowers, bursting into life from every patch of ground. From sand dunes and cliffs on the coast to the parched soil beneath ancient olive groves, hundreds of species can be found in a single week. Even roadside verges harbour an abundance of flowers; many alien species have been deliberately planted and grow

Alentejo favour many dry-country or semi-desert species of birds. Stone curlews, widespread throughout Europe, are common; while Calandra larks, black-bellied and pin-tailed sandgrouse have far more restricted distributions. Groves of cork oaks in the region support both little and Scop's owls, the latter most noticeable after dark, when they call, while isolated trees may hold a nest of

PEACE AND QUIET

quite readily alongside native grasses.

The geographical position of the Algarve and its resulting climate have had a profound influence upon both the flowering species of the region and their flowering period. Although not strictly part of the Mediterranean region, the Algarve has a distinctly Mediterranean climate, with hot, dry summers and mild, wet winters. However, the further west in the region you go, the greater the influence of the Atlantic, which moderates extremes in temperature and boosts rainfall.

In common with true Mediterranean regions, most plants flower in the spring, and many wither away above ground long before the height of summer. However, because of the moderating influence of the ocean, the flowering season extends over a far longer period, and more species can survive the hot summers intact.

The flowers of cistuses are a familiar sight in spring, looking like crumpled crêpe paper. Although the leaves of the many species found in the region are robust and often covered in a sticky or waxy coat, the petals are delicate and easily lost. Shrubs of cistus remain throughout the year, but many of the plants growing alongside them are either annual or appear above ground for only a few months in spring. The orchids of the region fall into this category, but their brief appearance is more than made up for by their attractive flowers.

Members of the bee orchid family, *Ophrys*, predominate, with yellow bee orchid and sawfly orchid being particularly common, but tongue orchids, bug orchid and naked man orchid can all be found by careful searching.

Rock roses, squills, tassel hyacinths, irises and clovers such as the starry clover add to the variety. They often grow amid great swathes of harestail grass, quaking grass and other species, whose seeds catch in your clothing with irritating frequency.

Open Country and Agricultural Land

Away from the coast of the Algarve, much of the rolling landscape is either covered in semi-natural scrub similar to the maquis vegetation of the Mediterranean region, or has been turned into agricultural land. Not surprisingly, the scrub is rich in natural history interest, and because the agriculture is anything but intensive, wildlife flourishes here as well.

The colourful and tangled scrub which often covers hillsides is an almost impenetrable barrier to larger animals, with the result that it is a haven for nesting songbirds. Sardinian, subalpine and Dartford warblers and goldfinches nest in its cover, the males sometimes singing from exposed perches to advertise their territories.

Wherever small pools of water persist into the summer months, birds from the parched scrub congregate to drink and bathe, often being far easier to observe there than they are away from the water.

Butterflies such as swallowtails,

Portugal is the largest exporter of cork in the world, and 90 per cent of the country's cork oak trees are in the Alentejo

scarce swallowtails, Cleopatras, fritillaries and blues visit the flowers and sometimes fall victim to the clutch of praying mantids. Chameleons also occur in scrub and among groves of trees, but their ability to change colour to match their surroundings makes them extremely difficult to spot. Groves and orchards of olive, carob, fig, orange and lemon are a familiar sight throughout the Algarve, but it is the almonds for which the region is especially famous. In January and February, the blossom on the almond trees is a wonderful sight and one which draws many visitors to the region.

Trees of all species harbour a wealth of insect life: the songs of cicadas and crickets are a constant reminder of their presence, but it takes a persistent search to find one of these elusive creatures. On the ground below, locusts and other grasshoppers bask in the sunshine and provide a ready supply of food for the hungry broods of woodchat shrikes which nest among the branches. Serins, too, share similar nest sites, but prefer to feed on seeds and smaller insects more suited to the size and shape of their bills.

As the olive and almond trees grow older, their appearance becomes more gnarled. The cracks and holes which develop are ideal nesting sites for little owls, which can sometimes be seen perched deep in the shade of the trees.

Bordeira

The dramatic cliffs of Cape St Vincent continue northwards up the western coast of the Algarve, battered along the entire length by the force of the Atlantic. Their height gradually moderates until, north of the town of Bordeira, the

PEACE AND QUIET

coast becomes dominated by sand. This fabulous area of unspoilt beaches and colourful dunes merges inland with areas of scrub, rich in wildlife. The whole area is a naturalist's paradise.

Beyond the Atlantic rollers, gannets file by on pure white wings, while terns plunge-dive for small fish closer to the shore. At all times of the year except the height of summer, small numbers of sanderling run along the shore at the very edge of the waves, catching small invertebrates; and groups of gulls roost above the tideline. The strandline is a rich source of food for scavengers, comprising the remains of dead animals and seaweed, and many land plants also benefit from this natural compost. Sea sandwort and the elegant sea knotgrass forms extensive mats over the debris and compacted sand and gravel.

As you move inland the flora becomes much more diverse, with the endemic thrift *Armeria pungens* forming large tussocks among the clumps of cistus and broom. Rockroses and the colourful cistus parasite *Cytinus hypocistus* adorn the sandy soil, and the brown bluebell *Dipcadi serotinum* and one-leaved scrub orchid can also be found. Where the vegetation is tall enough, the harsh scolding of Dartford warblers can be heard as they express their concern at intruders in their territory. Black-eared wheatears and stonechats stand alert on exposed perches, and bee-eaters dig their burrow nests in sandy banks.

The colourful array of flowers, which lasts from February until

Cork Oaks

Many of the trees of the Mediterranean and Iberia are evergreen, an adaptation to the climate of the region. One of the most characteristic and widespread species is the cork oak, so-named because of its thick, fleshy bark, which yields a rich crop of cork. The first harvest is generally taken after 12 to 15 years, the inferior quality of this first crop of cork resulting in its use in tanning. Thereafter, the trees yield a better crop, which is taken every 10 years or so, and they can produce as many as 15 harvests in their lifetime. Except when being harvested, cork oak groves are left largely to their own devices, and the lack of disturbance encourages birds like the serin, woodchat shrike, little owl and Scop's owl to nest. Although the trees are evergreen, their open canopy and the wide spacing of the trees allows a lot of light to penetrate to the rich growth of flowers in the understorey.

June, soon becomes parched and withered by the time the summer arrives. Before they wither, however, the flowers are a rich source of nectar for insects: bees, chafer beetles and butterflies such as fritillaries, blues and clouded yellows can all be seen. Not all the insect residents are quite so conspicuous or colourful: the subterranean mole cricket lives in underground burrows and seldom ventures out except at night or after heavy rains.

FOOD AND DRINK

Finding good, traditional,
Algarve cuisine these days is not
as easy as it used to be, which is
a great pity since, at its best, it is
truly excellent. There are several
reasons for its relative scarcity,
the chief of which is that, owing
to the boom in the tourist
industry, restaurateurs and
hoteliers have developed a type
of internationalised cuisine
designed to please most visitors.
If you want to try typical Algarve
cuisine, therefore, you will need
to go where the locals
themselves go, and in the

*A simple shady pavement café is an
ideal place to try the local dishes*

Algarve this generally means not
the hotels and restaurants in the
principal tourist resorts but
simpler establishments in the
small, inland towns and villages.
Elsewhere in southern Portugal
you will find a good selection of
simple restaurants serving
delicious food at very reasonable
prices.

Soups

In the Algarve and the rest of
southern Portugal soup can be
excellent or mediocre. Garlic

FOOD AND DRINK

soup, for instance, is traditionally drunk by the fishermen in the early morning, or as an accompaniment to grilled sardines. As an introduction to a meal it leaves a lot to be desired. Another soup to be wary of is the *sopa de peixe com massa*, which may be merely the water in which the fish has been cooked, with some form of rice and spaghetti added; it all depends on the quality of the fish stock and the seasoning.

The following soups, however, can be recommended, and all used to be commonly available, although once again the trend towards 'international' fare means that you may have to hunt them out.

● **Caldo de Grão**: this is a chickpea soup, popular in peasant diets, and eaten in various combinations with *massa*

Outdoor restaurants line the quay at Portimão and delicious fresh sardines come straight from the grill

(a type of pasta) or *chouriço* (sausage flavoured with garlic and paprika).

● **Caldo Verde**: a cabbage soup made by shredding the dark green *couve*, or Portuguese cabbage, boiling it briefly and blending it with a puree of potato and onions. It is particularly delicious when eaten with *pão de broa*, a bread made of rye and wheat flours.

● **Sopa de Agriões** (cress soup): one of the specialities of Portugal, this has a potato base with little else added except finely chopped onion with a little olive oil. The leaves of the cress are added in great quantities just before serving.

● **Caldeirada de peixe**: this is *the* Algarve speciality – a dish to which a great deal of thought and care is generally given. Similar to a *bouillabaisse*, it is often superior because it relies on better quality fish.

Among the other soups the visitor may encounter, *sopa de*

ervilhas (pea soup) is usually delicious, especially in spring. *Sopa de hortaliça*, a mixed vegetable soup, is also usually reliable, as is *sopa de feijão verde*, green bean soup.

Fish

● **Sardinha Grelhada** (or **Sardinha Assada**): one of the most characteristic Algarve dishes, grilled fresh sardines are best eaten straight from the charcoal grill with a salad and washed down with strong red Algarve wine. Once again, because of over-fishing and pollution, sardines are no longer so plentiful.

● **Salmonete** (red mullet): this is generally grilled and eaten with parsley and butter, though some ethnic restaurants serve it liberally sprinkled with garlic. It is now expensive, even in the simplest restaurants. A cheaper alternative is *besugo* which, if eaten in the same way as red mullet, is almost as good.

● **Tuna** (tunny): fresh tuna fish is something not to be missed in season. It is often fried with quantities of onions and served with chipped potatoes. Tuna preserved in brine and kept in large barrels can be eaten in a similar manner out of season.

● **Shellfish**: these are now very expensive compared with only a few years ago, but the diner will still encounter lobsters, crayfish and crabs and a whole range of smaller cousins for *hors d'oeuvres*. The lobster with big claws is called *lavagante* and is the more abundant and somewhat cheaper, while the crayfish type with longer feelers is *lagosta* (*lagostim* when small);

rather more expensive.
Other fish the visitor is likely to encounter, and which are usually grilled, include *cavala*, *sargo*, *carapau* and *solha*. The usual manner of dressing these is to dip them in a mixture of chopped garlic and olive oil before grilling. Small squid are called *lula*; the larger variety, cuttlefish, is known as *choco*, while octopus proper is called *polvo*. *Choco* is often served with oil and vinegar, having been cooked whole in water with onions, bay-leaf and marjoram. *Lulas recheadas* (stuffed squid) is a great Algarve speciality.

Staple Diet
A claim that is made of Portugal in general, and which certainly applies to the south, is that half the Portuguese diet consists of *bacalhau* (cod) and the other half of eggs. Furthermore cod, the national dish, is not the fresh variety one would expect of a country with 516 miles (830km) of Atlantic coastline, but is brought all the way from Newfoundland or from Norway, dried and salted. The Portuguese say there are 365 ways of serving it, to enable them to eat it every day without monotony. The favourite way is steamed with boiled potatoes or, more elaborate, stewed with potatoes, eggs and olives.

Meat
On the whole, meat dishes are not particularly memorable in this region of Portugal although the situation is saved by the

FOOD AND DRINK

excellent pork and fairly decent lamb. For those who cannot live without a steak, one of the best bets is *bifes de cebolada* – steak and onions cooked in a casserole with slivers of smoked ham, butter, white wine, parsley, seasoning and tomato puree. It is usually delicious and much more reliable than a straightforward grilled steak. Pork is served in a variety of forms, the most reliable being simply roasted, grilled or fried. Suckling pig (*leitão*) is usually good; for an unusual treat try pork with clams. Another worthwhile straight meat dish is *cordeiro assado* (roast lamb). This is lamb cooked in the oven, with lots of garlic stuck into the meat. Chicken is reliable, especially the simple *frango assado*, where it is turned on a spit over the charcoal brazier, and seasoned with pepper and garlic. *Frango piripiri* – joints of chicken marinated in a chilli sauce then barbecued – is probably the most popular tourist dish on the Algarve.

Bread
Algarvian bread is deliciously crusty. Baked in traditional wood-burning ovens, it is left with a fine dusting of ash on the loaves' bottoms. The wonderfully misshapen *pão caseiro* is the traditional loaf, while the wholemeal *pão integral* is favoured by the health-conscious and those who enjoy its nutty taste. The crisp golden bread roll, *papo seco*, is ideal for breakfast.

Cakes and Desserts
The cakes, sweets and conserves of southern Portugal, many of Arab origin, are usually excellent though excruciatingly sweet, particularly those made with figs, almonds and dried and candied fruit. Honey from the mountains here is especially delicious.

Among the specialities are *bolo real do Algarve* (made with sugar, almonds, egg yolks, covered with icing and bound with egg white) and *morgado de amêndoa do Algarve*, which is similar but more decorative. *Morgado de figos do Algarve*, a cake of dried figs, almond paste, sugar, chocolate, cinnamon and lemon peel is excellent. Rice pudding is also popular, and so is *pudim flan*, which is baked caramel custard.

Drink
The thing to drink in Portugal is wine. Not satisfied with the three normal shades – white (*branco*), rose (*rosado*) and red (*tinto*) – Portugal adds a fourth, green (*verde*). But the word describes its immaturity, not its colour. In fact, you can have a *vinho verde tinto* (green red wine). It is young wine of around 8 to 11 degrees of alcohol, still fermenting slightly in the bottle, and is grown inland from the Green Coast, the Costa Verde. It was the first of Portugal's wines to be exported, in the 15th century.

The other well known Portuguese wines are the Burgundy-type Dão, the dry white wine of Bucelas, the light white and red wines of Colares, and a wide variety from the banks of the Tejo. There are also sparkling wines from Lamego and Bairrada, and brandy. Portuguese liqueurs are worth trying: *bagaceira*, distilled from

Take the opportunity to try some of the excellent local wines

grape skins and pips; *medronho*, from the evergreen arbutus trees; and *cana*, from sugar cane. From Setúbal comes the sweet, fortified dessert wine *moscatel*, made from a mixture of black and white grapes.

Port

Perhaps the most famous of all Portuguese drinks is port. At one time it was drunk almost exclusively in England, but nowadays more than three times as much goes to France as to Britain. And the Portuguese themselves are acquiring a taste for it, though they prefer white port rather than sweet red, and as an aperitif.

Gone, too, are the days when the grapes were trodden by the foot. Now they are crushed mechanically and the *musto* is sealed up in metal or concrete tanks until the sugar content falls to the required level.

Of the different types of port, vintage port is made exclusively from grapes harvested in a particularly good year – on average, one in every five. After two or three years in bottle, the subsequent longer period of maturation takes place in wood. It throws a heavy crust or sediment, which clings to the side of the bottle and must be decanted. Some vintage ports may be drunk when they are only 10 years old, but they are often at their peak at 15 or 20 years.

Crusted port differs from the vintage in being a blend of two or three different vintages; it is aged rather longer in wood, maturing more quickly, but also spends a prolonged period in bottle and throws a crust or deposit, hence the name. It is lighter bodied, ready to drink in five to eight years, and less expensive than vintage port. Tawny port is a blend of different vintages, which undergoes lengthy maturing in cask. The bottle is in effect simply a decanter, and the lighter-coloured, more delicate wine is a favourite with people who find the vintage and crusted ports too taxing. The genuine article is by no means cheap, and fine old tawny is the wine which many of the shippers themselves most love. Late bottled vintage port is kept for up to five years in wood, but consists entirely of wine of the same vintage and develops a ruby colour and a vintage flavour and bouquet.

Ruby is a blend of relatively young wines matured in wood; it may greatly improve if kept in bottle for a few years.

Apart from these ports made from black grapes, there are also white wines, always matured in wood. These white ports were formerly sweet or very sweet, without the subtlety of the reds, but more recently the shippers have introduced dry white ports, made by fermenting out the grapes before brandying the wine, and are marketing them as aperitif wines.

Local Wines

The Algarve has a reputation for producing excellent grapes, along with acceptable local wines, particularly those from Lagoa and Lagos.

The local liqueurs, *medronho* – made from the arbutus berry – and *amêndoa amarga*, made from bitter almonds are worth trying.

SHOPPING

Owing to the huge increase in apartment and villa accommodation throughout the Algarve in recent years, the most enterprising of the supermarkets in the tourist areas are well stocked with foods imported from Britain and North America, although these imported goods are generally quite expensive. The principal markets in the region are in Olhão, Faro, Albufeira, Loulé, Armação de Pêra, Portimão and Vila Real de Santo António, where there are butchers, fishmongers, and endless stalls selling fresh fruits,

vegetables and herbs. (See individual entries for each town's market day.)

The following are the most worthwhile purchases for the visitor to southern Portugal.

- **Ceramics and tiles**: the Algarve is renowned for its local potteries, the best known of which are in Porches, which is noted for its fine traditional and original ware.

- **Leather**: Portuguese handbags, belts and shoes are of excellent quality and value.

- **Copper**: bowls, trays and lamps are locally made.

- **Cork**: Portugal is the largest exporter of cork in the world, and is famed for its cork products (see page 96).

- **Basketry**: little woven sisal baskets and hampers are available practically everywhere in the Algarve. You may still see women weaving the sisal fibres while sitting in the doorways of their houses.

- **Wines**: those with labels from Lagoa and Lagos are the Algarve's finest. The wines of the Alentejo are mostly heavy and high in alcohol content. Most of the vineyards are around Portalegre, Évora and Beja.

- **Confectionery**: sugary concoctions are made from almonds, eggs and figs, sometimes in elaborate shapes of flowers, birds, fishes etc. Each village has its own speciality. Other good buys are port, olive oil, all kinds of clothes, especially heavy-knit sweaters, articles of wood, pewter, brass and marble – the Alentejo has some of the largest deposits of marble in the world – hand-embroidered table cloths and bedspreads.

ACCOMMODATION

The Hotel do Golfe da Penina, Alvor, is one of several hotels with luxury leisure facilities

ACCOMMODATION

A wide variety of accommodation is available throughout the Algarve and southern Portugal, ranging from super luxurious 5-star establishments with international reputations and luxury villas and apartments, to simple pensions and campsites.

When a guest enters a Portuguese hotel he must be given a card showing the name of the hotel, the guest's name, the number of the room and its price (which cannot be changed during his stay), dates of arrival and envisaged departure, and the number of persons occupying the room. In accordance with international practice, the client, on registering, must indicate how long he or she intends staying in the hotel. Occupation of the room ends at midday.

Hotels must display, in a clearly

Hotel Gradings

The Portuguese hotel grading system follows the usual five to one star rating. Smaller hotels with fewer facilities are graded as *pensão* (pension) four to one star, or *residências. Estalagems* tend to be outside the main resort centres and offer good facilities, though on a small scale: they are rated four or five stars.

visible place, the prices charged for bed, Continental breakfast, lunch and dinner. The price of the room normally includes Continental breakfast. When a double room is occupied by one person the cost of one breakfast is deducted from the price. The prices include all charges and services. Children under eight are entitled to a discount of 50 per cent in all hotels if they share the room of the person accompanying them. Cots can be provided for babies if the hotel is notified when booking. Hotel prices, no longer

controlled by the state, vary
enormously. Generally rates are
higher in the Algarve and Lisbon
than the Alentejo. Bookings may
be made direct with the
establishment concerned or
through a travel agency. Tourist
offices maintain lists of
recommended accommodation.
One disturbing and increasingly
common practice is to squeeze
either a camp or sofa bed into a
room and then charge either an
under-occupancy supplement
when it remains empty, or the full
holiday cost to the unfortunate
trying to sleep on it.

Pousadas
Pousadas (government-owned
inns) are excellent value for
money and there are several in
southern Portugal. Usually
situated in places of great scenic
beauty, and often in beautiful and
sympathetically converted
castles, palaces, convents or
other historic buildings, a
pousada reflects the traditions,
art and cuisine of the region, or
historic site where it is located.
Advance bookings are strongly
recommended and can be made
through travel agents or directly
with the *pousada* organisation
ENATUR, Avenida Santa Joana
Princesa, 10, 1700 Lisboa (tel: 01
8489078).

Self Catering
There is a wide choice available,
especially in the Algarve,
ranging from luxury villas to
small, self-contained studio flats.
The development at Praia da Luz
is one of the earliest and best
developments, and that at
Vilamoura one of the biggest and
most luxurious.

Youth Hostels
There are youth hostels
(*pousadas de juventude*); two of
the best in the south are at

*A peaceful and shady whitewashed
villa – an ideal home for a fortnight
in the sun*

Sagres and Évora. Stays are
officially limited to three
consecutive days in any one
hostel, although this can
sometimes be extended if space
is available. (See also page 124.)

NIGHTLIFE AND ENTERTAINMENT

There are discothèques and
nightclubs (*boites*) throughout
the Algarve and southern
Portugal, varying from the
sophisticated to the simple to all-
night raves, and they generally
stay open until the early hours of
the morning. A number have
been grafted on to the local
scene, reflecting the nationalities
of their owners and aiming their

NIGHTLIFE AND ENTERTAINMENT

attractions at visitors from particular foreign countries. At many of those belonging to the bigger hotels you can alternately dance and watch the floor show. There are three casinos in the Algarve – at Praia da Rocha, Vilamoura and Monte Gordo – and all three have raised the standard of entertainment available to visitors, frequently presenting lavishly staged shows of international quality. All are quite conspicuous and easy to find.

Their hours of opening are standardised (17.00–04.00hrs) and, apart from the gaming rooms – offering *roulette*, blackjack, *baccarat* and French bank, as well as separate rooms with slot machines – they all have reasonable restaurants, bars and nightly floor shows. Casinos charge an entrance fee, and foreign visitors must produce their passports. Men are requested to dress smartly (but a tie is not usually necessary), at least in the evenings after 20.00 hours.

The Portuguese are a musical people and sing as they go about their work. Dancing at the country fairs and *romarias* is accompanied by song and almost every town or village of any size has a band.

Unique to Portugal is *fado* singing. This is a plaintive ballad, wailed rather than sung, of unrequited love, passion or despair.

The *fadista*, man or woman, wears black in memory of Maria Severa, the most famous and notorious of the early 19th-century singers, who died young. The song is usually accompanied by two guitarists. The audience listens in complete silence and then, when the last strange guttural note is wrung from the tense body of the singer, the response is usually wildly enthusiastic.

Kiss discothèque – one of many lively establishments popular with young visitors

WEATHER AND WHEN TO GO

The Algarve is popular as both a winter and summer holiday destination, being blessed with a mild year-round climate and very little rainfall. It is this dependability, of course, which makes the area a popular destination for outdoor sports enthusiasts. Sea temperatures tend to be colder than the Mediterranean, though the temperature of the sea in winter rarely drops below 59°F (15°C) thanks to the Gulf Stream. The water can also get a little rough and choppy, especially at the western end of the Algarve. In summer only light clothes are necessary for daytime wear and a pullover for cooler evenings. In winter it is best to take something warmer, while in spring and autumn lightweight clothes with a coat or wrap for the evenings are recommended.

In the larger hotels guests may change into more formal wear for dinner – but jackets and ties are rarely obligatory at the more up-market establishments.

On the beach, topless sun-bathing is common, but nude bathing is illegal throughout Portugal.

Apart from the Algarve, the remainder of southern Portugal tends to attract the majority of its visitors during the summer months, when the climate is mild and comfortable. The further north you travel the colder it becomes, with the result that the winter climate in Lisbon and the resorts on the Lisbon Coast is not nearly as pleasant as in the Algarve, in the extreme south.

HOW TO BE A LOCAL

The Portuguese are a reserved race who respond well to old-fashioned courtesies and polite manners. If you want to get to know them you may well have to make the first move, but once you have done so, you are likely

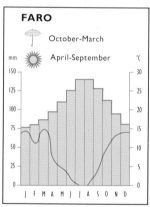

FARO

🌂 October-March

mm ☀️ April-September °C

to receive a warm response. Family life and ties are very important to the Portuguese and, being a strongly religious people, they tend to disapprove of overt sexuality in the form, for example, of nudism, so a respect for their customs, traditions and values is called for.

You certainly won't get to meet locals in places like Quarteira, Albufeira or the upmarket golf resorts around the Almansil area, as these are now almost solely north-European enclaves. But in the bars of Faro and other towns where ordinary people meet, it is not to hard to strike up a conversation.

Unfortunately, for the chances of meeting locals, the Portuguese do not have the same bar-crawling traditions that the British, Germans and Spanish do. Ask the tourist office, or at your hotel, which are the best places to get off the tourist track. They are not allowed to recommend any one place in particular, but they should give you a good idea where to go.

One area where you should *not* emulate the locals is on the road. They have one of the worst accident records in Europe. Remember that an extra degree of courtesy and patience may gain you a little more time and tolerance from drivers who may be characteristically impetuous and impatient.

Keep your wits and your temper!

CHILDREN

The Algarve is a good place for children. There are numerous safe, sandy, gently-shelving beaches where they can play without undue worry, and lots of water-based sports for older children: pedaloes, waterskiing, windsurfing, etc. Many hotels throughout the region have special children's swimming pools, and some have specific play areas.

The Algarve also boasts four water parks – Slide and Splash near Lagoa, The Big One near Alcantarillia, Atlantico Park and Aquashow, both near Quarteira, and there is also one between Beja and Serpa in the Alentejo. At all of these children can spend the entire day enjoying huge water slides, rapids, surf pools and many other water-based amusements and attractions. All the parks have restaurants and snack bars.

As in most southern European countries, children are made most welcome in restaurants and hotels, so there is no problem about taking them out with you to eat in the evenings. The mid-summer sun in southern Portugal can be quite fierce, so high factorprotection creams and hats are advisable for all children, and especially the very young. Remember that cots are not always easily available in hotels or self-catering accommodation. It is best to take a travel cot with you for very small children. Take your baby's usual brand of baby food from home, as it may not be available from the pharmacists in your resort. It is also a good idea to take disposable nappies with you, plus a first-aid kit that includes gripe water, pain-relief syrup and nappy-rash cream.

TIGHT BUDGET

Over the last few years the Algarve has become a mass-market holiday destination for north Europeans. This can work in one of two ways for those on a budget. While in many cases tourists are exploited, in others, competition is good for the holiday wallet, at least in the fast-food and cheap booze stakes. Here are a few tips to help your escudos go a little further:

• While charter flights are nearly always the cheapest way of getting to the Algarve, consider a last-minute cheap package deal too; you do not have to stay in the hotel allocated to you, and it may work out less expensive than a scheduled flight (but ask about special offers on these too). You can also use this as a starting point for exploring the rest of southern Portugal by public transport. Before you leave, ask the Portuguese National Tourist Office for details on train and bus passes.

● Always try to get off the beaten track for the cheapest accommodation and meals. You will not find fancy international cooking in the villages, but neither will you pay fancy international prices. Follow the locals for the best deals.

● Beware of fish and shellfish that is priced by weight. A good restaurant will always weigh the item you have chosen and tell you in advance how much it will cost. If they do not, you must ask. Shellfish in particular can be exorbitant.

● Even in the resorts you should be able to find cheap *residencias* or *pensaos*. Ask at the tourist office. Tourist office staff are usually a valuable source of knowledge on the accommodation situation. Or consider camping (see **Camping** page 114).

● If you are self-catering, buy your food from the village markets, and have a picnic instead of lunching out. Buy your holiday souvenirs here too. Haggling is allowed on non-food items.

SPECIAL EVENTS
Carnival
In February, in the week before Lent, great celebrations are held in various towns and hamlets of the Algarve and southern Portugal. The town of Loulé, in particular, is the setting for particularly animated revelry and street activity.

Algarve Music Festival
During May and June, concerts and recitals are held throughout the region, as well as performances by the Gulbenkian Ballet.

Beer Festival, Silves
In June, there is a chance to sample all the brands of beer produced in Portugal, to the accompaniment of folk-dance groups and musicians.

Facatil Handicrafts Fair
Held in August at Lagoa, this major fair has crafts from the whole of Portugal on display and for sale.

National Folklore Festival
This is a colourful and lively event, one of the most important folk festivals in Portugal. Groups from all parts of the country participate, particularly in Lagoa and Tavira. (September)

Penina International Jumping Competition
One of the country's premier show-jumping events, attracting top Portuguese and international riders. (September)

International Algarve Car Rally
One of the most important sporting events in the Algarve takes place October to November throughout the whole region.

The Algarve Tourist Board produces a monthly calendar of events; look out for it in hotels, restaurants, etc.

SPORTS

Portugal has established a well deserved reputation for being a paradise for sportsmen and sportswomen, and nowhere is the reputation more deserved than in the Algarve, where the weather seldom stops play and where visitors can practise favourite sports year-round.

Fishing

More than 200 varieties of fish are to be fond in Portuguese waters. Even from the beach there is every chance of landing sole, plaice, bream or bass, although fishing off these waters is not easy. There is particularly good fishing from rocks and from cliff-tops, but extreme care is required in case of sudden wind or misjudgement. At greater depth skate, mackerel and tuna can be caught. The ideal time for anglers is from the beginning of October to mid-January, when

The Algarve climate makes golf one of the region's greatest attractions: there are many outstanding courses from which to choose

the seas are rougher.

Big Game Fishing: the main centres for this type of fishing are Vilamoura and Portimão, where enthusiasts can join regularly organised fishing trips and where they can also hire the necessary equipment.

Underwater Fishing: the whole coast is good for diving, with the waters bordering the west coast of the Algarve particularly transparent. Those who wish to practice aqualung diving should note that they are not permitted to use a gun or any other fishing device. Spear fishing is allowed only when no artificial breathing apparatus is used; even so, the minimum distance from the beach must be 164 feet (50m), and a marker buoy is obligatory.

Golf

The Algarve is without doubt one of the most popular destinations

in Europe for golfing enthusiasts, offering the chance to tee-off on some of the best maintained and most challenging courses anywhere on the globe, and also to enjoy high standards of accommodation and food at reasonable prices. A year-round warm climate ensures that practically any time is the right time to hit the fairway in the Algarve.

The main golf courses in the region are Palmares, which enjoys a lovely location near Lagos; Parque da Floresta; Penina; the Pine Cliffs, set within the Pine Cliffs Golf and Country Club near Albufeira; the San Lorenzo, within the same complex as the Quinta do Lago course; Vale do Milho, at Carvoeiro; Vilamoura I; Vilamoura II; Vilamoura III; Vale do Lobo; and Quinta do Lago.

Palmares: in a setting of 550 acres (222ha) at Meja Praia, Lagos (tel: (082) 762953), Palmares is considered to be one of the most scenic golf courses in the Algarve, commanding wonderful views over the bay of Lagos and the distant Monchique hills.
The golf course is surrounded by a complex of villas, apartments, an aparthotel and the 4-star Hotel Golfino, plus swimming pools, tennis courts and a shopping centre.

Parque da Floresta: designed by Pepé Gancedo, several times Amateur Champion of Spain and creator of other well regarded courses, Parque da Floresta, thanks to the improved road system, is now within easy reach

of any part of the Algarve that one might choose as a holiday base: at Budens, 10 miles (16km) west of Lagos (tel: (082) 65333). The par-72, 6,942-yard (5,888m) course is set in hilly countryside with some dramatic holes necessitating drives over yawning chasms and pitch shots over water-guarded greens.

Penina, Montes de Alvor, Portimão (tel: (082) 415415): the Penina estate consists of an 18-hole championship golf course designed by the late Henry Cotton and two nine-hole courses. The par-73 championship course, which has been chosen for innumerable major competitions and tournaments, is spread over landscaped grounds with waterways and lakes forming a major feature of the design.

Pine Cliffs: a nine-hole course designed by English golf architects Hawtree & Sons to be as demanding as any leading 18-hole course.

San Lorenzo (tel: (089) 396534): the 18-hole 72-par San Lorenzo championship course is one of the Algarve's newest. It was designed by the American Joseph Lee in conjunction with William 'Rocky' Roquemore and is situated in a 2,000-acre (810ha) estate at Quinta do Lago, already renowned for its abundant wildlife. The 27-hole Quinta do Lago course is within the same complex.
San Lorenzo is owned by Trusthouse Forte which is building a new 5-star hotel overlooking the 18th green. In

the meantime, guests staying at the nearby Hotel Dona Filipa can play San Lorenzo free, while guests at the Hotel Golfe da Penina pay 50 per cent of the green fee.

Quinta do Lago: the 27-hole Quinta do Lago course is spread over nearly 300 acres (121ha) and was designed by the late American golf course architect William Mitchell. The three nine-hole loops which are set in picturesque terrain of pine trees and artificial lakes have been hailed as among the ten best courses in Europe because of the excellence of their design and the standard of maintenance. Close to Almansil, a nine and a quarter mile (15km) drive from Faro Airport, the complex has attracted a number of international property development companies which have provided high quality homes. Facilities for the golfer and holiday-maker include windsurfing on the lagoon, horse-riding, tennis courts, saunas and a swimming pool. (Tel: (089) 394529.)

Vale do Lobo (tel: (089) 394444): designed by the late Henry Cotton, Vale do Lobo has one of the most photographed holes in Europe – the long par-3 seventh on the Yellow Course, which stretches from the tee over two ravines to the green 210 yards (192m) away.

Vale do Milho: designed by former Ryder Cup player David Thomas, this 9-hole par-3 course is set in the Jorge de Lagos Village and Country Club,

Carvoeiro. (Tel: (082) 358502).

Vilamoura I: this par-73 course, which opened in 1969, has been laid out along the lines of the classic English courses and offers scenic beauty that has few parallels in European golf. It is 6,924 yards (6,331m) long and set among gentle pine-clad slopes, with the sea providing a spectacular backdrop. (Tel: (089) 313652.)

Vilamoura II: designed by the English architect Frank Pennink, this attractive par-72 18-hole course was opened in 1976 and was formerly known as the Dom Pedro.
The course measures 6,808 yards (6,225m) and the first nine holes are on open land, with magnificent sea views, while the back nine wind home through umbrella pines climbing gently towards the clubhouse.
There is a restaurant open from 07.30hrs until midnight. (Tel: (089) 315562.)

Vilamoura III: a true American-style course laid out by Joseph Lee. A coastal setting for 27 challenging holes, many with tricky water hazards. Lessons are given and there is a restaurant. (Tel: (089) 380724).

Horse-riding
The Algarve's climate and countryside is ideal for horse-riding and there are several stables which cater for it. Experienced riders will find both the Portuguese Lusitano and the Anglo-Arab stocks. Learners are also provided for and there are ponies for children.

SPORTS

Brightly coloured windsurf sails are a common sight on Algarve beaches

The principal stables are West Algarve Riding Centre, Burgau (tel: (082) 65152); Quinta da Balaia (tel: (089) 55787); Pine Trees at Quinta do Lago (tel: (089) 394369); Quinta dos Amigos (tel: (089) 95636); Vilamoura (tel: (089) 314675); Carvoeiro (Casa Pegasus) (tel: (082) 57262); and Quinta da Saudade at Guia (tel: (089) 56182).

Sailing

The Algarve offers the sailor excellent opportunities, from remote coves in which to drop anchor and relax, to full service marinas such as that at Vilamoura: picturesque fishing ports; and a wide choice of on-shore facilities. Enthusiasts can hire a dinghy or charter a yacht to experience the excitement of sailing the Atlantic in Mediterranean-like weather. Yachts can be chartered from the Carvoeiro Club (tel: (082) 357266), while many large hotels have facilities for sailing.

As well as the open sea, there are lagoons along the coast at Faro, Olhão, Tavira, Portimão, and Vila Real de Santo António, which are ideal for sailing.

Tennis

The Roger Taylor Tennis Centre, at Vale do Lobo (tel: (089) 394779) is one of Europe's top tennis centres, with six of its 12 (soon to be extended to 20) all-weather courts floodlit. The David Lloyd Tennis Centre, in a lovely setting at Carvoeiro (tel: (082) 358856), has ten all-weather courts, five of which are floodlit, and other superb facilities.

Though not on the same grand scale, the Algarve has several other tennis centres.

DIRECTORY

Contents

Arriving

Visas

Visas are not required for holders of British, Irish, US and Canadian passports, for visits of up to 60 days (Australian and New Zealand passport holders – 90 days). This period may be extended before expiry by application to the Foreigners' Registration Service, Rua Conselheiro Jose Silvestre Riberio 22, Lisbon 1600 (tel: (01) 7141027), or go to the District Police HQ seven days before the original period elapses.

By Air

Several airlines, notably TAP Air Portugal in conjunction with British Airways, operate scheduled services to Faro Airport, although the majority of holiday-makers arrive on charter flights.

To cope with the increased flow of holiday-makers to the Algarve, a new 3 million passenger capacity terminal has been opened at Faro Airport, which is located about four and a quarter miles (7km) – 15 minutes – from Faro, the regional capital. The new terminal cost £15 million to build, and is now the most modern in Portugal (tel: (089) 818281). It has 25 check-in desks and is equipped with sophisticated passenger handling, flow control, security and communications systems. And in addition to the usual fast-food outlets, restaurant, duty-free shopping, banking and medical facilities, special provision has been made for children, handicapped and elderly passengers, with the designation of special areas. Most package tours to the Algarve include transport between Faro Airport and your accommodation. For independent travellers, there are buses (number 16) from the airport to Faro town, approximately every 45 minutes between 08.00 and 20.00hrs. Taxis also make the journey.

By Road

Only those with a considerable amount of time at their disposal take their own vehicles to southern Portugal . The distance from the French port of Calais to Lisbon, for example, is around 1,300 miles (2,100km), usually requiring three of four overnight

DIRECTORY

stops. To reduce the drive, those motorists who do use their own cars can send them on by freight train from Paris to Lisbon, while passengers travel by the 'Sud Express' sleeper train, which operates daily in summer and takes about 25 hours. You can then take the motorail service from Lisbon to Faro (summer only), or continue your journey by car – it is a three or four hour drive from Lisbon to the Algarve. Alternatively, there is a car ferry between Plymouth (England) and Santander (northern Spain) twice a week in summer – crossing time about 24 hours, details from Brittany Ferries in England (tel: 0752 221321). The drive from Santander to Lisbon is about 580 miles (934km).

Fly/Drive

Fly/Drive holidays to the Algarve are proving increasingly popular and arrangements are now widely available at Faro. The cost can be substantially reduced if four passengers go together. The rates usually include the flight, hire of the car on an unlimited mileage basis, and sometimes accommodation for the first and final nights of the holiday.

Camping

There are excellent large campsites with good amenities at Albufeira, Alvor, Armação de Pêra (two sites), Faro, Lagos (two sites), Monte Gordo (two sites), Olhão (two sites), Portimão, Praia de Luz, Quarteira and Tavira. Stick to official campsites (*parques de campismo*), of which there are many in the Algarve, some even offer furnished chalets for rent. Off-site camping is permitted but is not advisable.

An International Camping Carnet is compulsory on sites belonging to the Federação Portuguesa de Campismo; on other sites it is recommended. The Portuguese National Tourist Office publishes a guide, *Roteiro Campista*, detailing campsites throughout the country; it is available from the PNTO and bookshops in your own country. Additional information can be obtained from Federação Portuguesa de Campismo, Rua Voz do Operário 1, 1000 Lisbon (tel: (01) 8862350).

Chemists (see Pharmacies)

Crime

Crime, nearly always petty theft, is sadly starting to become as common on the Algarve as in neighbouring Spain. Theft from hire-cars is rife, so never leave anything of value, even in a locked boot, for any amount of time in an unattended car. Lisbon is notorious for the Fagin-like dexterity of its pickpockets, so be very careful there at all times. It is best to avoid the Metro completely. As in any big city, certain quarters and streets should also be avoided at night. Be careful in the Alfama and Bairro Alto districts.

Customs Regulations

Visitors from Europe may bring in limited quantities of certain duty-free goods, as shown below (slightly more generous allowances if tax and duty have been paid in EC countries): 200 cigarettes or 100 cigarillos or 50 cigars or 250g of tobacco; 1 litre spirits, 2 litres of drinks 22 per cent or less alcohol, plus 2 litres wine; 50g perfume; 0.25g toilet

Traditional transport; a curiosity for the visitor, but a hazard when driving on unfamiliar roads

water. Duty-free allowances for those living outside Europe are the same as above, except the tobacco allowance, which is doubled. In common with other EC countries, VAT on certain items may be reclaimed by non-residents. Small quantities of tea and coffee may be brought in. However, it is forbidden to import fresh meat into Portugal. If you are carrying items of obvious high value, you may find it useful to carry the receipt as proof that duty has been paid.

Driving

To drive in Portugal you must have a valid national driving licence and the vehicle registration document. If the car is not registered in your name a special certificate, authorising you to use the car, is required. Also, an international motor insurance certificate, or Green Card, though not compulsory, is strongly advised.

The minimum age at which a visitor may use a temporarily imported car, or motorcycle (over 50cc), is 17 years. However, as the minimum age to hold a driving licence in Portugal is 18, visiting UK or Republic of Ireland driving licence holders under 18 may encounter local difficulties.

In Portugal they drive on the right and overtake on the left. The rules of the road are similar to other Continental countries. Portuguese motorists themselves are not noted for their driving

DIRECTORY

skills, so extra care is required. The wearing of seat belts is compulsory and children under the age of 12 cannot travel in the front seat unless fitted with a child restraint; there are heavy fines for those who infringe these laws.

The use of a warning triangle is compulsory in the event of an accident or breakdown, and must be placed 33 yards (30m) back along the road.

Speed Limits

Speed limits, unless otherwise stated, are 37mph (60kph) in built-up areas and 56mph (90kph) on other roads, except motorways where the limit is 74mph (120kph).

Breakdowns

Orange SOS telephones are located on the main highways, and the national motoring club, Automóvel Clube de Portugal (ACP), operates a breakdown service. Assistance may be obtained in the south of the country by dialling (01) 9425095. If you find yourself in the north of the country you should call (02) 316732. If more serious, the emergency number 115 is for police and ambulance.

Car Rental

To rent a car you must be 23 or over and have possessed a valid national or international licence for at least a year.

All major international car rental companies are well represented, competing with numerous small local firms whose rates are often cheaper, but who must be approached warily since their vehicles are not necessarily as reliable.

Auto Jardim (largest car rental company in Portugal). Main office: Avenida da Liberdade, Edificio Brisa, 8200 Albufeira (tel: (089) 512415).
Auto Universo (a reliable local company). Main office: Rua de S Gonçalo de Lagos 15, 8000 Faro (tel: (089) 22862); Faro Airport (tel: (089) 27010)
Avis Faro Airport (tel: (089) 818538)
Budget Cerro Grande, Albufeira (tel: (089) 54997)
Europcar Estrada Aeroporto, Montenegro, Faro (tel: (089) 818777); Faro Airport (tel: (089) 818316)

Fuel

There are two grades of leaded petrol: normal (85 octane) and super (98 octane); unleaded fuel – *gasolina sem chembo* – is sold as super (95 octane). Away from the main roads, filling stations tend to be scarce, so it is sensible to keep the tank well topped up.

Credit cards are accepted as payment in most places, but a tax of 100 *escudos* is added to the cost when petrol is paid for in this way.

Electricity

The current throughout southern Portugal is 220 volts AC and sockets accommodate the circular two-pin Continental-style plug.

In the majority of hotels and the more up-market villas there are shaving points which take the British-style two-pin plug, but you should take an adaptor (North American visitors a voltage transformer) with you if you intend to use other electrical appliances.

Embassies and Consulates

Embassies (all in Lisbon; telephone code 01):
Australia: Avenida da Liberdade 244 (tel: 523350)
Britain: Rua de São Domingos à Lapa 35-37 (tel: 661191)
Canada: Rua Rosa Araùjo 2, (tel: 563821)
Eire: (Consulate) Rua da Imprensa (tel: 3961569)
US: Avenida das Forças Armadas (tel: 7266600)
British Consulates: Rua Santa Isabel 21, Portimão (tel: (082) 23071); Rua General Humberto Delgado 4, Vila Real de Santo António (tel: (081) 43729).

Emergency

The national public emergency service telephone number is 115. Dial this if you need police, fire or ambulance.

Health

No inoculation certificates are required for visitors to Portugal from non-infected countries.

The twin towers of Lisbon's Sé (Cathedral) with blue skies and exotic palms

Nationals of the European Community can benefit from treatment under the state health service. To qualify, an EC passport or form E111 is required. If you need medical treatment, go to a health centre – *Centro de Saúde* (the local tourist office should be able to give you the address) – and ask the doctor, who will want to see your passport or E111, to be treated under EC arrangements. Patients may be charged from 20 to 65 per cent of the cost of prescribed medicines, and the full cost of some medicines. Hospital treatment is normally free, but you may have to pay for secondary examinations, X-rays for instance.
Dental treatment is very limited under the state scheme; you will probably have to pay and these

charges are not refundable.
The cost of medical treatment in
Portugal makes travel insurance
essential if you are a non-EC
citizen, and recommended for
all. For medical treatment and
medicines, keep all bills to claim
the money back later from your
insurance company.

If your ailment is a minor one,
pharmacies (*farmácias*) can give
advice and prescribe medicines.

Holidays (Public)

Shops, banks and offices are
normally closed on the following
days:

1 January New Year's Day
February – Tuesday the week
before Lent, Carnival Day
March/April Good Friday
25 April Revolution Day
1 May Labour Day
May/June Feast of Corpus Christi
10 June Portugal Day
15 August Feast of the
Assumption
5 October Republic Day
1 November All Saints' Day
1 December Independence Day
8 December Feast of the
Immaculate Conception
25 December Christmas Day

Lost Property

If you are robbed or lose
anything while on holiday in
Portugal, report it immediately to
the police (Policia de Segurança
Pública). It is important to obtain
a written statement from them
that you have done so, for many
insurance companies make this a
condition for accepting your
claim. If you are travelling with a
group, the travel company's
representative should also be
informed.

In Lisbon, for objects lost in the
street, contact the police in Rua
dos Anjos; for objects lost in a
tram or bus go to the property
department in the Largo do
Carmo, beside the Santa Justa lift
(tel: (01) 3465035). If objects are
lost in the underground, go to the
lost property department in
Restauradores underground
station (tel: (01) 3427707).

Media

The English-language
publications, the fortnightly
Algarve News (obtainable from
tourist offices) and the monthly
Algarve Magazine, contain
listings and articles on things to
do and see in the region,
including special events, local
festivals, restaurants and nightlife
in bars, pubs and clubs all along
the coast.

Foreign newspapers and
periodicals are widely available
in all the major holiday resorts.
Portuguese Radio (*Radiodifusão
Portuguesa*) has two principal
stations: *RDP 1* transmits on 383
and 451 metres medium wave,
and *RDP 2* on 290 and 397
metres, also on medium wave.
Emergency messages to tourists
are broadcast in English every
hour during the news, Monday to
Saturday, from July to
September.

Money Matters

The Portuguese unit of currency
is the *escudo*, divided into 100
centavos, and its symbol – the
dollar sign – is written between
the *escudo* and *centavo* units.
One thousand *escudos* is known
as a *conto*.

Banknotes are issued for 50, 100,
500, 1,000, 2,000 and 5,000
escudos; coins for 1, 2 1/2, 5, 10,
20, 25, 50, 100 and 200 *escudos*
and 50 *centavos*.

Banks are open from 08.30 to 15.00hrs Monday to Friday, although the bank at Vilamoura marina is open daily from 09.00 to 21.00hrs. Credit cards and travellers' cheques are accepted in many hotels, restaurants and shops, and most hotels will exchange currency and travellers' cheques outside banking hours. Exchange bureaux (*serviço de câmbio*) are found in Lisbon and the major resorts, with varying opening hours, in many cases seven days a week.

Currency Regulations

Visitors may import up to 100,000 *escudos*, and an unlimited amount of foreign currency, though amounts in excess of the equivalent of 500,000 *escudos* must be declared on arrival. The minimum which visitors entering Portugal should possess is 10,000 *escudos*, plus a further 2,000 *escudos* for each day of their intended stay; these can be equivalent amounts in other currencies.

No more than 100,000 *escudos* in Portuguese currency may be taken out of the country, but there are no limits to the amount of foreign currency which may be exported, providing it was declared on entry.

Opening Times

Shops: usually open from 09.00 to 13.00hrs and again from 15.00 to 19.00hrs, Mondays to Fridays, and 09.00 to 13.00hrs on Saturdays, although many of the newer shopping centres and supermarkets, especially in the larger resorts, remain open until much later, and also open on Sundays.

Banks: (see **Money Matters**)
Post Offices: (See **Post Offices**)

A rainbow of fresh and dried flowers for sale – just one colourful aspect of the local scene in Portugal's capital city

DIRECTORY

Offices: normal office hours are from 09.00 to 17.00hrs, with one hour for lunch between 13.00 and 14.00hrs.

Museums: as a general rule, museums open from 10.00 to 17.00hrs, though some close for lunch and are open from 10.00 to 12.30hrs and again from 14.00 to 17.00hrs. Most museums are closed on Mondays and on public holidays, of which there are many (see page 118). It is advisable to check with a tourist office before visiting. The vast majority of museums charge an entrance fee, except on Sundays. Palaces in Lisbon close on Tuesdays.

Churches: open early in the morning but are often closed during the afternoon between 13.00 and 16.00hrs, opening again in the evening.

Personal Safety

All hotels are required by law to have fire exits with signs, fire prevention apparatus and fire instructions, and the majority of hotels in southern Portugal abide by the law. But sometimes smaller hotels are not so careful with their safety equipment, so visitors are advised to identify the nearest fire exit and see if it is open, check where the nearest fire appliance is in relation to their room, and read the fire safety instructions.

As is the case in many holiday areas in Europe, hotels in southern Portugal use different lifts to the kind you may be used to. In newer hotels lifts have an internal door as a rule, but in many of the older establishments they do not, and these three-sided lifts are a cause for concern, especially where children are involved. Since they have no inner door, passengers run the risk of abrasion or worse against the wall as the lift ascends or descends. Because of the potential risk involved, parents should not allow children to use them unaccompanied.

Cliffs and sandy bays are among the scenic attractions of the Algarve, but it is important to take extra care near the cliffs and steep slopes and prevent children from climbing.

Some of the new villa and resort developments are poorly lit at night, so the use of a small pocket torch could prevent a sprained ankle.

Swimming Pools/Bathing: Portuguese hotels are not, in general, as safety conscious around the pool as many others, so close supervision of children is suggested. Most pools give little indication as to which is the deep end and which the shallow end.

Pharmacies

Chemists (*farmácias*) usually prescribe for minor ailments or put you in touch with a doctor for more serious matters. They are open during normal shopping hours.

At other times one chemist in each neighbourhood is always on duty round the clock. Hall porters, tourist information offices and police stations will direct you to the *farmácia do turno* or duty chemist. You will find the address, however, displayed in the windows of all closed chemists' shops and it also appears in local newspapers.

Places of Worship

Anglican: Family services of Holy Communion are held every Sunday at various resorts and villages in the Algarve. Members of all denominations are welcome. English-language services are held regularly at St Ana's Church, Albufeira; Nossa Senhora de Fátima, near Almansil; and St Andrew's, Penina.

Roman Catholic: Masses are held in every village and town throughout the region, with regular English-language services at St Andrew's, Penina.

Baptist: Services are held regularly at Avenida 25 Abril, Lote 17, Portimão.

Police

Police who wear red armbands marked 'CD' are assigned to assist holiday-makers and usually speak several foreign

Our Lady of the Rocks chapel, with its wonderful setting on the cliffs above Armação de Pêra

languages. The Guarda Nacional da República (GNR) patrol the roads in white cars or on motorbikes, and carry out spot checks on documents.
In case of emergency, telephone 115.

Post Offices

Local post offices are usually open from 09.00 to 18.00hrs, Monday to Friday, and main post offices from 08.30 to 18.00hrs, or even 18.30hrs, Monday to Friday. Main offices are also open on Saturday mornings; they can be found in Faro, at Largo do Carmo; in Lagos, at Rua Porta de Portugal; and Portimão, at Avenida Dom Afonso Henriques. Lisbon's main post office, situated in the Restauradores, is

DIRECTORY

open 24 hours. They can be identified by the letters CTT, and offer similar services to those in other European countries.
You can also buy postage stamps (*selos*) at souvenir stands and shops such as tobacconists, if they display the sign *correios*.

Public Transport

Air
LAR Air Services operate domestic flights between

Take the easy way to the top: Lisbon is built on hills so trams make exploring easier

Lisbon/Faro/Portimão/Vila Real de Santo António and other airports to the north, as well as charter flights covering 20 airports throughout the Portuguese mainland.

Rail
Portuguese Railways (known as CP) provide an extensive network of services throughout the country. Trains, however, can be infrequent and slow. Some trains are steam-operated but even some of the diesels are not known for their swiftness. There is an express service between

Lisbon and the Algarve, the *Sotavento*, which leaves Lisbon daily for the four-hour journey.Fares are relatively inexpensive and various discounts apply.
Ask about the *Cheque-Trem* card which enables the holder to a 10 per cent discount on all tickets and is valid for an unlimited period. There are also 'blue period' (*períodos azul*) discounts for trips of more than 62 miles (100km). The *Cartão Jovem* provides a 50 per cent discount for trips of more than 31 miles (50km), while the *Cartão Família* gives reductions to families on round-trip fares.
Passengers should note that it is obligatory to pay before travelling and that they must have a valid ticket before boarding any train, or risk substantial on-the-spot fines.

Bus/Coach
The national bus/coach line *Eva Transportes* provides a faster, more frequent and more comfortable (though costlier) service than trains. There are daily coach services between Lisbon and the Algarve, taking around five hours, and express services between major cities. Local bus services (*autocarros*) run to even the smallest villages. A bus stop is known as a *paragem*. Local buses offer a convenient and inexpensive way to see some of the more out of the way places of the region. Schedules are available from transport operators, local tourist offices or travel agencies.

Taxis
Taxis, recognised by their black livery and green roofs, can be

A few miles inland from the sea, traditional Algarve life goes on as always

found at specific ranks, and there is usually at least one rank in most major towns and resorts. The majority of taxis follow a standard fare based on kilometres travelled which is usually displayed inside the cab. If it is not, you can ask the driver to show you the rates.

Tipping is not compulsory but is usual – about 10 per cent of the fare is considered appropriate.

Senior Citizens

Southern Portugal, especially the Algarve, is a popular holiday destination with all age groups, but a particular favourite with older holiday-makers, especially those who enjoy golf. Many elderly people have retired to the Algarve or have bought holiday homes there so they can enjoy the climate and facilities for more than just a couple of weeks at a time. In consequence, the region is used to welcoming the middle aged and elderly, and this is reflected in the many shops and stores catering specially for their needs and preferences.

Senior citizens who are able to travel to southern Portugal out of the peak summer months can also find many travel bargains. Low-cost flight-only deals are available, and it is often possible to rent a villa or apartment for an extended winter stay for a fraction of the high season price. Hotels, too, offer extremely attractive rates to elderly people staying for several weeks at a time. Senior citizens (over 65) can benefit from 50 per cent reductions on the fares of Portuguese Railways, on production of a Eurorail Senior Card (details from travel agents in your home country).

Student and Youth Travel

Air travel offers the best deals; rail is more flexible. The Inter-Rail ticket is valid in Portugal for

DIRECTORY

A familiar sight to British visitors, this post box would look more at home in London than Lisbon

those under 26 years of age. Children under four travel free and from four to 12 pay half fare. (Full details are available from mainline stations in Portugal.) Young tourists (aged 14 plus) can stay in dormitories (*pousadas de juventude*) at very low rates if they are members of a national or International Youth Hostel Association. More information can be obtained from the Associação Portuguesa de Juventude, Rua Andrade Corvo 46, 1000 Lisbon (tel: (01) 539725).

Telephones

Calls can be made from any main post office, some of which will handle the call for you and collect the cost afterwards, or you can dial direct from a public telephone booth, or the call may be made by the hotel's receptionist and then taken in your room, but for this service there is an additional charge. For international direct dial calls use the code 00 for calls within Europe and 097 for the rest of the world, followed by the country code: 44 for the UK, 353 for Eire, 1 for the US and Canada, 61 for Australia, and 64 for New Zealand, followed by the area code (remembering to drop the initial 0), then the required number. Coins for local calls are 5, 10 or 20 *escudos*; for national and international calls use 50 *escudos* coins. Some phones will only accept phone cards.

Time

From the last Sunday in September to the last Sunday in March, the time in Portugal is GMT plus one hour. During the summer it is GMT plus two hours. So for most of the year, Britain is an hour ahead of Portugal; New York and Montreal are six hours behind Portuguese time; Sydney nine hours ahead and New Zealand 11 hours ahead of Portuguese time.

Tipping

Although a service charge is included in hotel, restaurant and café bills, it is still customary to tip. A reasonable amount would be eight or ten per cent. This would be appropriate for hairdressers, too. It is also customary to tip taxi-drivers by perhaps slightly more than that. Public lavatory attendants also expect a small tip, as do hotel porters carrying your luggage.

Toilets

The standards of hygiene and cleanliness, including those in lavatories, are higher in Portugal than in many other holiday destinations. Lavatories are marked *homens* (men) and *senhoras* (women), or use internationally-recognised symbols.

Tourist Offices

Before you travel, useful information can be obtained from the Portuguese National Tourist Office.

UK: 22-25A Sackville Street, London W1X 1DE (tel: 071 494 1441).

US: 548 Fifth Avenue, New York, NY 10036 (tel: 212 354 4403); Suite 3001, 919 North Michigan Avenue, Chicago, IL 60611 (tel: 312 236 6603); Suite 616, 3440 Wilshire Boulevard, Los Angeles, CA 90010 (tel: 213 380 6459).

Canada: 60 Bloor Street, West Suite 1005, Toronto, Ontario M4W 3B8 (tel: 416 921 7376); Suite 1150, 1801 McGill College Avenue, Montreal, Quebec H3A 2N4 (tel: 514 282 1264).

Australia and New Zealand: refer to London or New York offices.

Further information on the Algarve may be obtained from the Algarve Tourist Board, Rua Ataíde de Oliveira 100, 8000 Faro (tel: (089) 803667-71), or from separate tourist offices in the region (see under individual resorts for addresses and telephone numbers).

Have your shoes shined on the Avenida da Liberdade, Lisbon, but don't forget the tip

LANGUAGE

Everyday Phrases

good morning bom dia
good afternoon boa tarde
good night boa noite
please faz favor
thank you obrigado; *or, if you are
a woman*, obrigada
I'd like queria
yes/no sim/não
how much? quanto custa?
I'm sorry desculpe
not at all de nada
goodbye adeus
can you direct me to.. pode
indicar-me o caminho para...
to the right à direita
to the left à esquerda
do you speak English? fala
inglês?
I don't understand não entendo

While Travelling/Sightseeing

airport aeroporto
bathroom quarto de banho
beach praia
bread shop padaria
bridge ponte
bus station estação de autocarros
bus stop paragem
cake shop pastelaria
campsite parque de campismo
cathedral sé
chapel capela
chemist farmácia
church igreja
farm quinta
fish shop peixaria
fountain fonte
garage garagem
garden jardím
greengrocer hortaliceiro
house casa
inn estalagem
library biblioteca
market mercado
men homens
monastery mosteiro
museum museu

palace palácio or paço
park parque
petrol/gasoline gasolina
petrol station posto de gasolina
police station posto de policia
post office correio
quay cais
railway station estação de
caminho
restaurant restaurante or tasca
shower banho de chuveiro
spa estância termal
square praça
supermarket supermercado
swimming pool piscina
telephone telefone
telephone kiosk cabina telefónica
theatre teatro
tobacconist tabacaria
tourist information poste de
turismo
town centre centro cidade
town hall câmara municipal
women senhoras

Food and Drink

breakfast pequeno almoço
lunch almoço
dinner jantar
tea (meal) lanche
the bill a conta
is the service included? o serviço
está incluido?
the wine list a lista dos vinhos
bread pão
cheese queijo
chicken frango
coffee (small black) bica
coffee (white) café con leite
eggs ovos
fish peixe
ham fiambre
lamb anho
orange juice sumo d'aranja
pork porco
steak bife
tea chà
veal vitela
water (with gas) água (com gaz)

INDEX/ACKNOWLEDGEMENTS

Acknowledgements

The Automobile Association would like to thank the following photographers and libraries for their assistance in the preparation of this book.

MALCOLM BIRKITT took all the photographs not listed below (AA Photo Library).

AA PHOTO LIBRARY (J E Edmansun) Bags and purses, 16.

J ALLAN CASH PHOTO LIBRARY 83 Cathedral, Lisbon, 112 Windsurfers.

NATURE PHOTOGRAPHERS LTD 87 Ponta da Piedade, 88 Saltmarsh broomrape (P R Sterry), 90 Arneria Pungens (K J Carlson), 90 Cistus Albidus (B Burbidge), 92 Azure-winged magpie (M Bolton), 93 Great bustard, 95 Cork oak (K J Carlson).

SPECTRUM COLOUR LIBRARY 62 Monastery of Jerónimos, 67 *Fado* singers, 73 Estoril, 78 Royal Palace, Sintra, 101 Vineyard, 124 Post box.